humble
STRENGTH

The Eye-Opening Benefits of Humility

KEVIN VOST

ASCENSION

West Chester, Pennsylvania

Ascension
PO Box 1990
West Chester, PA 19380
1-800-376-0520
ascensionpress.com

Cover design: Allison McEvoy

Printed in United States of America

22 23 24 25 26 5 4 3 2 1

978-1-954881-31-0 (paperback)
978-1-954881-32-7 (e-book)

CONTENTS

Introduction

WHY ON EARTH SHOULD WE STRIVE TO GROW IN HUMILITY?

In Paradise there are many Saints who never gave alms on earth: their poverty justified them. There are many Saints who never mortified their bodies by fasting or wearing hair shirts: their bodily infirmities excused them. There are many Saints too who were not virgins: their vocation was otherwise. But in Paradise there is no Saint who was not humble.[1]

—Fr. Cajetan Mary da Bergamo

Thus humility is, as it were, a disposition to man's untrammeled access to spiritual and divine goods.[2]

—St. Thomas Aquinas

Christ calls us *all* to strive to become saints, so that one day we will enjoy eternal bliss in heaven with him and with the glorious communion of saints. Now saints, even the ones officially canonized by the Church,

1

though humble to a man and woman, come in all shapes, sizes—and temperaments, too. Let's start off by examining a few of them in action.

False and True Humility: From Muddy Boots to Flowering Fruits

In the sixteenth century, St. Philip Neri was so loved for his zeal for Christ and his role in the spiritual renewal of Rome, he became known as "the Apostle to Rome," much like a second St. Peter. So joyous was his demeanor that he is also known as the patron saint of mirth. (Now that's my kind of saint!) Yet, he could get down to serious business when it came to defending the Faith—and rooting out false humility.

The great twentieth-century Catholic psychologist Henri Joly tells the story of the time the pope asked Philip to go to a monastery and meet a sister who, it was said, had received private revelations. It happened to be wet weather, but Philip made the trip to the monastery on his mule. Once he reached his destination, "the sister was brought to him and she appeared full of sweetness and unction." The tired, soggy priest then took a seat, sticking out his boot and asking the sister to pull the boot off his foot. It didn't take him long to draw his conclusions. When the sister reacted to his request with disdain, "he seized his hat and went back to the Vatican, to tell the Holy Father that a religious, so devoid of humility, could not possibly possess the graces and virtues she was credited with."[3] Notice how important *humility* is to the saints!

Joly tells another story of a priest who, like St. Philip, needed to investigate whether a certain woman was truly receiving extraordinary spiritual gifts as she claimed. "'You are the saint, aren't you?' he said to her. 'Yes, Father,' was the answer he got. The illusion was instantly detected."[4] Pride is destroyed by true humility, as *real* saints know.

Thérèse of Lisieux reacted very differently to someone who suggested that she possessed great holiness. She replied, "No, I am not a Saint. I have never wrought the works of a Saint. *I am but a tiny soul whom Almighty God has loaded with His favours.* The truth of what I say will be made known to you in Heaven."[5] This humble young woman once wrote to God in her diary how she strove to "scatter flowers" to him:

To scatter flowers!—that means each sacrifice:
My lightest sighs and pains, my heaviest, saddest hours,
My hopes, my joys, my prayers—I will not count the price—
Behold my flowers![6]

She understood so well how the simplest, humblest, most mundane acts we perform every day, if done for God's sake, become acts of beauty and love. Thérèse scattered flowers to God whether she was scrubbing floors or bearing up patiently with the most annoying behaviors of the most irksome sisters in the whole convent! Though she did not leave her cloister and died at the age of twenty-four in 1897, she would be canonized in 1925 and become known around the world as St. Thérèse of Lisieux, "the Little Flower." (My own family and I were for several years members of one of the many "St. Therese, the Little Flower" parishes spread throughout the world.)

Therese had true humility. Having no pretensions about her own saintliness, she focused what she thought were her meager talents and aimed them directly at God and her neighbors. Her humility not only helped raise *her* to sainthood, it continues to raise *us* all up to this day, through her writings, her example, and her willingness to intercede for all who would pray to her.[7] In 1997 St. John Paul II officially declared her a great "Doctor" (teacher) of the Church, an elite group of thirty-six saints, only four of whom are women (so far).

So we can see from these little stories that we must beware of embracing pride (masquerading as *false humility*), and should strive to move toward the real thing. And yet in our modern, secular times, *many people question even the value of true humility itself.* That being the case, let's take the time in the introduction of this practical guide to humility to carefully "define our terms," as logicians (and philosophical Church Doctors like St. Thomas Aquinas) would surely advise us to do. We will start with what humility *isn't* and then take our first peek at just what it *is*.

What Humility Is Not

There are all kinds of misconceptions about the nature of humility, what it is, and about the kinds of thoughts, emotions, and behaviors it produces. A modern secular business book addresses typical misconceptions of humility in our current American culture, including the idea that humility means "being meek or being subdued or thinking that you're not a worthy person."[8] The authors believe this derives from common synonyms including "*lowliness, meekness,* and *submissiveness*—characteristics that would seem to be the antithesis of achievement and success."[9]

Distinguished psychologists Christopher Peterson and Martin Seligman include a chapter on humility in their well-received psychological handbook from 2004, *Character Strengths and Virtues*, in which they also describe common misconceptions of humility in our modern secular world. They note that "humility and modesty are easily misunderstood in the contemporary United States, where we are encouraged to be full of pride and brimming with self-esteem and self-importance." Indeed, they feel the need to make clear that "to be humble and modest does not entail self-derogation or self-humiliation," and further, that "these traits do not mark a person as a loser, a shrinking violet, or a depressive."[10] (Following their lead, we did *not* subtitle this book on humility "How to Become a Loser, a Shrinking Violet, or a Depressive.")

Still, many people today do unfortunately associate humility with feelings of low self-esteem at best, or self-loathing at worst, implying that if you are a humble person, you do not feel that you have what it takes to be successful or happy, and therefore you act meekly and submissively toward others; or that you do not feel worthy of happiness and success, and therefore you believe it fitting to wallow in lowliness and abandon any efforts toward joy and fulfillment in life.

I've seen atheists attack the very notion of Christian humility, drawing their ammunition from some striking biblical verses like this one: "But I am a worm, and no man" (Psalm 22:6). To be a good Christian, these atheists proclaim, is to despise oneself like a worm, a surefire guide to low self-esteem and a life full of misery, bereft of achievement and happiness.

Recall too, if you will, the great drive to enhance school children's "self-esteem" in recent decades. I remember from teaching developmental psychology courses in the 1990s that some international studies on grade-school students showed that while American students, on average, performed significantly worse than students of many other countries in tests of academic subjects like math, our students "won" in self-reported measures of "math self-esteem." In other words, the kids from the US felt very good about themselves and very confident about wonderful mathematical abilities *they did not possess!*

It appeared that through well-intended but misguided efforts to conquer feelings of low self-esteem, teachers taught children to think better of themselves *without knowing themselves as they really were*, both in the recognition of the capacities they truly possessed and in the recognition of capacities they had not yet actually developed. To cut to the chase just a bit, humility helps every one of us know our own strengths and our weaknesses better, so that our beliefs better match our reality and our performance better matches our self-expectations. Further, when we grasp with humility our own true deficiencies, we are far more likely to do something about them to become competent in things that deeply matter in life.

What Humility Is

So let's begin to look at the benefits of true humility and just what humility *truly* is! For one thing, humility is a *virtue*, a perfection of the powers God gives us as human beings. It is a lowly virtue in some senses, but awesomely lofty in others. Twentieth-century Catholic thinker Dietrich von Hildebrand declared that "humility is the precondition and basic presupposition for the genuineness, the beauty, and the truth of all virtue."[11]

Humility is a virtue intimately tied to *truth* and *reality.* According to St. Thomas Aquinas, humans experience truth when our conceptions or beliefs about reality correspond to or match with reality itself. A person with true humility will certainly not be over-confident in abilities he or she does not possess, but neither will he or she lack confidence in the God-given talents he or she truly does possess—and has worked diligently to cultivate over time (for practice is required to perfect any virtue).

One of humility's most basic roles is indeed to ground us in reality, and yes, I literally mean "ground." Our English word humility derives from the Latin *humilitas,* which itself is related to *humus,* meaning earth, ground, land, or soil. Humility's connotations of lowliness are thus quite accurate—humility is, in a sense, as low as the dirt beneath our feet! So then, just how does "lowly" humility rate as among the most important and desirable of all human virtues? Good question. Here's a first attempt at an answer.

When we act humbly, exercising humility, we recognize our true place in the hierarchy of God's universe. Recalling that the word humility is related to humus, we should consider that the very word *human* is related to it as well! Indeed, though we were formed from the lowly soil, we *are* exalted above all animal and plant life on earth. And yet we were created a "little" lower than the angels (see Psalm 8:5), and needless to say, we are infinitely lower than the God who created us all.

So what of the previously cited Scripture verse that compared men to worms? Well, like worms and all forms of life, we do get our start in the humus of the earth, but we must also bear in mind the context of these words. In his doleful twenty-second psalm of praise to God, King David begins with most memorable words: "My God, my God, why have you forsaken me?" (They are so memorable because Jesus Christ remembered them and uttered them from the Cross. See Matthew 27:46 and Mark 15:34.) They mark words of lamentation during incredible trials. David metaphorically calls himself a worm and not a man right *after* he has praised the holiness of God and right *before* he reports that he has been the object of scorn, spite, and mockery from other men. He expresses his anguish, feeling like less than a man, but he immediately recalls that even when he was his smallest and weakest, within his mother's womb, almighty God loved him and kept him safe.

To compare oneself to a worm does not mean to loathe one's very existence but to willingly humble oneself in awe of the benevolent majesty of God, who is infinitely higher and holier. Such humility leads not to self-loathing and misery but to *solace* in the fact that, despite our humble origins, God is truly always with us. It leads to *gratitude* for God's bountiful outpouring of love and blessings upon us—if we are but humble enough to recognize and welcome them. (Still, we thought it best *not* to entitle this book "How to Be a Worm.")

Within the realm of humanity as comprised of unique, individual human beings, the humble recognize that while *all* of us have been given great gifts from God, foremost among them our very existence, we don't decide who receives which *particular* temperaments, talents, gifts, and potentialities for achievement or success in various endeavors. That's up to God's providence. The humble will thank God for whatever he has given us without selfishly begrudging it when it appears he has given greater gifts to others. St. Paul tells us as much: "Do nothing from selfishness or conceit, but in humility count others better than yourselves" (Philippians 2:3).

Not only does humility enable us to rejoice in the excellence of others, humility is the *virtue* that prepares the ground for virtually every other virtue or human excellence in us. And not only does humility help us *grow in virtue*, it is a most powerful ally in helping us *conquer sin*. Indeed, we will discover in the pages ahead precisely how humility can help us conquer the seven deadly sins, and even the "queen of the vices" herself, who commands them all. We will look closely at the specific thoughts, emotions, and behaviors that manifest these sins in our daily lives so we can accurately examine our own consciences and know just where and when to send humility forth for us in battle. Indeed, we will come to see how humility is among the most powerful weapons we can wield in the spiritual warfare against Satan and his prowling evil minions and also against the inclinations toward sin within our own souls. We will learn how to keep this humble but mighty weapon sharp and ever ready at hand.

When we grow in humility by accepting God's grace and training ourselves every day to think, feel, and act in truly humble ways, this realistic acceptance of all of our weaknesses and sinfulness, as well as all of our potentialities for greatness and holiness, will unlock our full capacities to live as God intended us by making us in his image and likeness. In fact, if we take literally our hypothetical question of why "on earth" we should strive for humility, there are all kinds of earthly reasons.

Earthly Reasons to Cherish Humility

Peterson and Seligman note that the character trait of humility is marked by "honesty and authenticity," is "fulfilling," and is "associated with acceptance of oneself and an appreciation of one's place in the larger world." It "is highly valued, if not always in ourselves then certainly in others," and, indeed, "this character strength elevates others."[12]

Business professor Edward D. Hess and researcher Katherine Ludwig, in *Humility Is the New Smart*, wrote in 2017 that humility is the "hero" of their story on how to succeed in a rapidly changing electronic business world, calling humility "the gateway to human excellence."[13]

The humble do not rest on their laurels as the world passes them by. Rather, they remain ever ready to learn new things from others, new ways of looking at things, and new ways of getting new jobs done. Such humility not only leads to all kinds of earthly benefits for the humble themselves, it enables them to rise up and do good for those whom they love.

Heavenly Reasons to Grow in Humility

Above earthly reasons (both literally and figuratively) are the *heavenly* reasons why we should strive to grow in humility. As we saw in our opening quotation, almost eight hundred years before our modern psychologists and business professionals sang paeans to praise the earthly benefits of humility, the Angelic Doctor declared that humility can provide us a disposition to "untrammeled access to spiritual and divine goods."

Many Catholic thinkers throughout the ages have strongly emphasized the spiritual and divine benefits of the virtue of humility.

In *Humility: Wellspring of Virtue*, Dietrich von Hildebrand wrote as follows: "On the degree of our humility depends the measure in which we shall achieve freedom to participate in God's life and make it possible for the supernatural life received in holy Baptism to unfold in our souls."[14] In describing humility as the wellspring of virtue, he echoed St. Thomas' statement that humility provides "untrammeled access to spiritual and divine goods"—indeed, even the highest good of all, the beatific vision of God someday in heaven. And speaking of heaven, von Hildebrand also notes that "humility implies a heavenward aspiration that carries with it a breath of greatness and holy audacity."[15] Humility stands ready to help us ascend—all the way to heaven!

As to that heavenward aspiration of humility, in the classic *Humility of Heart*, Fr. Cajetan Mary da Bergamo (1672–1753), a humble Capuchin, wrote in his very first lines that there were many saints, who, due to their particular circumstances or vocation, never gave alms, never wore hair shirts, and were not virgins: "But in Paradise there is no Saint who was not humble."[16] All the saints were humble because they so loved and patterned their lives, whatever their circumstances or callings, after the humility of *Christ*.

Indeed, Jesus Christ explicitly told us: "Come to me, all who labor and are heavy laden, and I will give you rest. Take my yoke upon you, and learn from me; for I am gentle and lowly in heart, and you will find rest for your souls. For my yoke is easy, and my burden is light" (Matthew 11:28–29). Further: "Whoever humbles himself like this child, he is the greatest in the kingdom of heaven" (Matthew 18:4), and: "For every one who exalts himself will be humbled, and he who humbles himself will be exalted" (Luke 14:11). Christ's call to humility could hardly be clearer (though he did indeed, for our sake, repeat and clarify this call again and again, as reported in other Gospel passages we will visit in the pages ahead).

All Christians would do well to heed the advice of the Protestant minister Andrew Murray, who believed that humility is a sadly overlooked virtue that should be front and center in the life of every Christian who strives to follow Christ. Murray wrote, "We must make humility the chief thing we admire in Him, the chief thing we ask of Him, and the one thing for which we sacrifice all else."[17] Just think of that, *humility* considered the chief, number one priority thing. The "him," of course, is Jesus Christ, and I hope and pray that this book too will inspire such a passionate zeal for humility in imitation of and love for Jesus Christ in you (and in me, too, since I may have far more to learn about practicing humility than you do).

How This Book Works (or at Least Gives It Its Best Shot)

Humility's Assembly Manual

If we are to build humility within our souls, we need to know not only *why* we should want to built it, but also *what* we are building—and *how* to build it!

An old photo from a warm summer day in the late 1980s shows me lying with my back on the ground, hands on my knees, face glowing red. I'm straining to leg press a heavy wooden beam into just the right position as two handy grandpas quickly bolt it to two other beams. You see, I am not the mechanically handiest guy, while my father and father-in-law sure were. Thankfully, they insisted on helping me put together their grandson's heavy-duty swing set. (They would be the brains and I would provide the brawn.) By the time I had perused the first page or two of instructions, the grandpas already had the thing half together. Unfortunately, they hadn't looked at the instructions at all, and having gotten one of the steps backwards, they called in my legs and my back to jam things together in place, rather than taking everything apart and starting over.

It all worked out in the end that day, but in my experience, that was the exception to the rule. Have any of you ever had to take apart a piece of something you thought you had put together correctly and had to redo a step or two before you moved on?

Well, if we are to build humility within our souls, we will do so most effectively, and with the fewest mistakes and backtracking, if we carefully read its assembly directions first! So what do we find within a good assembly manual?

- PARTS: There will be a description and picture of the necessary parts. That's just what you'll find in our first three chapters. Humility undergirds all the virtues, and per St. Thomas, all virtues consist of "parts." We'll find out just what parts we need to use and just how humility helps us put each and every part together.

- TOOLS: Thankfully, God has given every one of us both the *natural tools* (inborn uniquely human capacities) and *supernatural tools* (like prayer, the sacraments, and a myriad of graces including the seven gifts of the Holy Spirit) we need to put humble lives together. We'll put these tools to use in every chapter.

- WARNINGS! Depending on the product, some instructions will include warnings. Do this or that wrong and you might have to start all over again—or even end up getting electrocuted! After all, some missteps can even be deadly. Well, all of our chapters, and especially the fourth, will be full of warnings, namely, the *vices* and *sins* we must avoid if we are to grow in humility, and instructions on how humility can keep help our souls safe from them. For indeed, at least seven of these sins are deadly to humility and deadly to our souls.

- STEP-BY-STEP INSTRUCTIONS: Of course, every good assembly manual guides us through the process with step-by-step instructions. You will find them here in chapters 5 and 6 (with steps that were written by great saints, no less). We'll examine St. Benedict's twelve steps of humility and St. Anselm's seven steps up the mountain of humility, both in the light of St. Thomas Aquinas' analyses.

- PICTURE OF ASSEMBLED PRODUCT: Finally, if our instructions are good ones, we'll be shown a picture of the completely assembled end product, our goal, the reason we've learned all the parts, headed all the warnings, used the right tools, and taken all the steps. *The end product of humility is to be like Christ*, who is displayed front and center in chapter 7.

A Few Specifics on What Lies Ahead

In the chapters that follow you will encounter a myriad of the *spiritual and divine* goods that come from humility, and indeed quite a few *earthly* benefits as well. We'll answer all kinds of intriguing questions like these, some of which you may (or may not) have thought about before:

- How does humility open up our minds to reality and truth?

- How does humility help us conquer our greatest fears?

- How does lowly humility square with Jesus' call to let our lights shine before men and to multiply our talents?

- In what ways does Christ literally embody humility, and how can we live out his invitation to become humble like him?

- How does humility hold the keys both to limited earthly happiness and to eternal joy in heaven?

And for fun, but for spiritual insights as well, we'll also tackle some questions like these that I'm pretty sure have *not* crossed your mind before:

- If *Pride* and *Justice* were teammates in a chariot race against *Sin* and *Humility*, which team would win, and why? St. John Chrysostom and St. Thomas Aquinas knew, and when you get to chapter 2, you will too.

- If *Pride* and *Deceit* faced *Lowliness* and *Hope* on an open field of battle, which side would emerge victorious, and why? Aurelius Prudentius Clemens and St. Thomas knew, and when you get to chapter 4, you will too, and you'll learn even more (like who Prudentius was!).

Oh, and last, but certainly not least (a question the entire books strives to answer):

- Exactly how can *I* practice humility, grow more humble, and hopefully influence my loved ones to practice and grow in humility with me?

Humility Personified

I'll try not to get too abstract in the pages ahead, so let's start with something concrete. Have you ever heard of "reification"? It comes from the Latin words *res* for "thing" and *facere* for "make" and involves treating something abstract as if it were a concrete thing. A quick example that comes to my mind (especially around St. Valentine's Day) is using a heart to represent love. Well, at times we'll do something a little like that for humility and the virtues it supports, but we'll take the process one step further—and higher, to make humility a little easier to understand, while honoring "her" at the same time!

Let me show you what I mean. In the book of Proverbs, *Wisdom* is repeatedly personified and spoken of as if "she" were a righteous woman.[18] For example, a passage in the very first chapter begins, "Wisdom cries aloud in the street; in the markets she raises her voice" (Proverbs 1:20) before she expounds on various counsels, reproofs, and warnings. The personification intensifies as Wisdom testifies "she" was there "when he [God] established the heavens" (Proverbs 8:27).

"Wisdom" in Greek is *sophia*, from which we get the word "philosophy": *philia* (love) of *sophia* (wisdom). While the great Catholic thinker Boethius awaited his death sentence in a sixth-century Italian prison cell, he penned his magnificent book *The Consolation of Philosophy*, in which "Lady Philosophy," another personification of wisdom, comes to offer him solace.

Now, though I could certainly not wax as eloquent as King Solomon or Boethius if I wanted to, please note that we may personify *humility* now and again in the pages ahead (including our chapter titles) with phrases like "humility says ..." or "humility does ..." It's a step toward trying to bring humility to life, foremost of all in our own lives.

Humility in Person(s)

A key element of the pages that follow will be to show how humility is indeed literally personified, that is, *made incarnate within the hearts and souls, thoughts and actions, of real live human beings* (because we want to make it grow in our own hearts and souls, too). Therefore, get ready for lots of stories of humility in action. They are mostly true stories (and I'll tell you when we encounter fictional or fictionalized accounts, just in case they're not obvious, like when we get to the sad, soggy tale of the monkey and the dolphin).

When we see the precise ways humility is lived in the lives of others, it will *inform* us about what we need to do to grow in humility, *inspire* us to make humility our own, and *transform* our hearts and souls. Oftentimes, we'll start each chapter section with a little humility vignette, and then dig in deep to unearth all its lessons.

One More Thing: Humility Lived Saint Stories

Lest I forget, while each chapter will be liberally peppered with great insights and anecdotes of the saints (and a fair sampling of sinners), each chapter will end with a "Humility Lived Saint Story." We've seen twice now already that Fr. Cajetan Mary da Bergamo said every single saint was humble. In these brief essays we will highlight one saint from a host of possibilities to show just how he or she lived out humility as addressed in the previous chapter's specific theme. Got favorite saints of your own? Then perhaps you might guess as you read through each chapter which saint might be found at its end.

Humility, the lowliest virtue of them all, can cast from our paths all obstacles to the highest of all good things: a humbler, happier, holier life on earth as we prepare to meet and enjoy Good with a capital G in heaven.

Now, let's get down to business and grow more humble together, the good Lord willing, of course!

PART I

Humility Undergirds Virtues

Christ is the first to tell us, at the end of the Sermon on the Mount, that we must build our spiritual edifice not on sand, but on a rock, and St. Paul adds that the rock is Christ Himself on whom everything must rest.

To build this temple we must, therefore, dig the foundation until we find the rock. According to St. Augustine, the excavation symbolizes humility, which is, says St. Thomas, a fundamental virtue.[19]

—Fr. Reginald Garrigou-Lagrange

The great twentieth-century Thomist[20] theologian Fr. Reginald Garrigou-Lagrange argued that *humility is the base upon which all virtues rest,* humility itself resting upon the immovable rock of Jesus Christ. Indeed, in his wonderful writings on growth in the spiritual life, Fr. Garrigou-Lagrange compared the development of Christian spirituality to the construction of a holy temple, and he provided a helpful model that we will strive to keep in mind as we move through the three chapters of this book's first part.

Building a Temple of Humility and Love

Fr. Garrigou-Lagrange's spiritual temple image is built upon a solid rock, who is Jesus Christ. It depicts humility as the base of the temple. Humility provides the foundation for the *moral virtues*, especially the four *cardinal virtues* of prudence, justice, fortitude, and temperance, that hold secure the doors (*cardo* being Latin for "hinge") that lead to a host of other virtues and gifts of the Holy Spirit. Indeed, humility is also the base upon which pillars of the loftiest of all virtues rest, the God-infused *theological virtues* of faith and hope, with charity (or love), the greatest and most enduring of all virtues, as the overarching dome. Further, humility grounds lamps of holy light that emerge from faith, hope, and charity—the Holy Spirit's *gifts* of understanding, knowledge, and wisdom at the apex. These supernatural gifts perfect the three *intellectual virtues* of the same names.

So then, in our first three chapters we will see how humility lays the groundwork for a host of natural and God-given virtues and gifts that perfect the human soul as it *seeks truth*, *does good*, and *loves God*. We will find that humility, though lowly and meek, is anything but weak—a veritable spiritual Atlas that not only holds up the earth on its back, but which helps us grasp hold of God's "strong hand and ... outstretched arm" (Psalm 136:12) that makes any burden light.

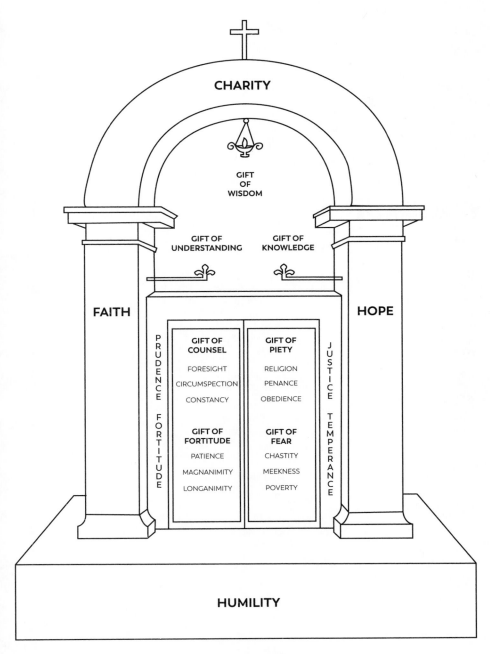

Chapter 1

HUMILITY SEEKS TRUTH

Learn from me; for I am gentle and lowly in heart,
and you will find rest for your souls. For my yoke is easy,
and my burden is light.

—Matthew 11:29-30

Let the children come to me, and do not hinder them;
for to such belongs the kingdom of heaven.

—Matthew 19:14

Christ bids us to learn from him, with gentleness and humility as his first and foremost lesson. If we trust in him, follow him, and imitate him, we will be in the best position to allow him to teach us everything worth knowing. In fact, our very capacity to learn, to come to know facts of reality, understand their meanings, and use this information wisely to guide our own lives manifests the wonderful natural gift of the human intellect, the fundamental reason we are unique among all creatures on earth, having been made in the image and likeness of God (though at an infinitely more humble level!).

Christ *Is* the Truth Humility Seeks

Note that Christ, who *is* Truth itself (see John 14:6), immediately ties learning to humility.[21] If we are gruff and full of ourselves, rather than gentle and lowly in heart, we are in a poor position to learn new things from others, or even to be aware that we have so much to learn. Further, we may lack the desire to learn what is *real* or *true*, being concerned to learn only what might advance our own selfish desires or make us look good in the eyes of others.

We have been made to seek Truth, from the time God knit each one of us in our mother's wombs (see Psalm 139:13). From the moment we emerge from the womb, we are called to "grow in the grace and knowledge of our Lord and Savior Jesus Christ" (2 Peter 3:18). Indeed, St. Peter bids us, "Like newborn infants, long for the pure spiritual milk, that by it you may grow up to salvation" (1 Peter 2:2). We must also seek to grow in the maturity of our knowledge to become spiritually suited for the "solid food" of Christ's teachings (see 1 Corinthians 3:2; Hebrews 5:11-14). Our hunger for Christ's truth should grow and be fed throughout every stage of our lifespan on earth, and "he who endures to the end will be saved" (Matthew 24:13).

St. Thomas tells us that all virtues are firm habits that start as "dispositions," tendencies we build within ourselves to think, feel, and act in specific ways, through repeated practice. Further, he frames them in a developmental perspective: "a disposition becomes a habit, just as a boy becomes a man."[22] Let's take a look now at some stories that show how the virtue of humility can grow within each of us, just as a child becomes an adult, helping us seek and find truth throughout all the seasons of our life on earth.

Humility Seeks Truth: The Little Boy Who Asked, "What is God?"

"What is God?" "What is God?" "What is God?" The brilliant, though perhaps annoying child, never tired of asking the poor Benedictine monks of the monastery of Monte Cassino this less-than-easy question. He had been entrusted to their care at about the age of five, but he had always acted this way with a wholly holy thirst for truth. Even as a toddler, one day when his mother took him to the baths of Naples, he grabbed up a sheet of paper and refused to let it go, bawling when anyone tried to make him. On the paper was the Hail Mary, and in the interest of peace and quiet, his mother let him take it to the bath. An early biographer wrote that this young boy could be kept from wailing only by letting him hold a paper with writing.[23]

Perhaps the boy learned a little more from the way each monk answered his question about God, and throughout the rest of his life, he never stopped asking the question—and illuminating the world with some very brilliant answers of his own. The little boy with an unquenchable thirst for the truth of God would later be known and loved as the Church's Angelic Doctor, Doctor of the Eucharist, Doctor of Humanity, and Common Doctor (that is, common to all throughout the Church)—St. Thomas Aquinas. And come to think of it, one day he would preach sermons and write commentaries on every line of the Hail Mary prayer as well![24]

God clearly gifted Thomas with an unusually powerful intellect, but, outside of God's graces, nothing led to its perfection like the great saint's *intellectual humility*. He always knew there was so much about God and the splendors of his creation that he did *not* know, so he constantly asked questions of others and paid close attention to their answers. Indeed, he is often praised as the foremost among all of the Church's great Doctors, and here is a key reason why.

In the sixteenth century, Cardinal Thomas Cajetan said of Thomas that because "he most venerated the ancient doctors of the Church, [he] in a certain way seems to have inherited the intellect of all."[25] And popes into our own time have agreed! Read any page from Thomas' great *Summa Theologica* (summary of theology), and you will find it peppered with direct quotations from dozens upon dozens of Eastern and Western Church Doctors, saints, and theologians. Indeed, when you read Thomas, you are reading almost every great mind and soul who came before him!

Now, following in Thomas' large footsteps and becoming the thirty-seventh Church Doctor may not be on your bucket list. Yet if the extraordinarily gifted Thomas could embrace intellectual humility, acknowledge the limits of his knowledge, ask others to help him understand, listen carefully to their answers, remember, and apply them, maybe we too can do all within our own unique capacities to harness such humility to grow in *our* knowledge and love of God.

Understanding Humility

The mature St. Thomas described our intellectual power of *understanding* as the capacity to "penetrate into the heart of things," to grasp things as they truly are. Indeed, the word "intellect," a synonym for understanding, derives from the Latin words *intus* for "inside" and *legere* for "read"; in essence, to read what's inside.[26] Humility helps us do just that, to see things as they really are, down deep, and not just as we would wish them to be, since the humble place truth above their selfish wishes as they seek true understanding. So let's try to understand what lies deep down at the heart of humility itself.

In our introduction, we already touched a bit upon the etymology of our English word humility and how it is related to the Latin *humilitas*, which itself is related to *humus*, meaning earth or ground. The Greeks used the word *tapeinos*, which literally means "low to the ground" and figuratively means "humble." Note the commonality of meaning with the Latin and how it also relates to a common English synonym of humility, namely "lowliness." Indeed, in one of his great calls to humility that started our chapter, Christ calls himself "lowly in heart" (Matthew 11:29).

So, to understand humility we must grasp its essence in terms of the word's earthly and lowly origins, and yet, as Christians, our understanding can penetrate deeper "into the heart" of humility than the wisest of secular Greeks and Romans were able to do.

Through natural reason, the Greeks, Romans, and other early peoples were able to deduce that humans do indeed come from the earth, live our lives on it, and at the end of our days return to its soils. Further, they were also aware that behaviors born of an overweening, excessive pride and haughtiness (*hubris* for the Greeks and *arrogantia* for the Romans), were an affront to "the gods" and often led those who displayed them, and sometimes their friends and families, toward disaster. Therefore, they recognized some value, at times, in a measure of humility, though humility was rarely counted among the chief virtues in ancient secular cultures (in which virtue was primarily connected with a manly self-confidence and self-assertion).

It was God's interactions with man, made through his revelation and recorded in the Scriptures, that provide us with the fullest understanding of the essence of humility. We learn in the first chapter of Genesis that our common father, Adam, was indeed fashioned from "dust from the ground" by God, who "breathed into his nostrils the breath of life; and man became a living soul" (Genesis 2:7).

So then, here are our first fundamental *God-revealed* clues to the essence of humility. Not only do we derive from the humus of the earth, as reason tells us, but we, the earth itself, and everything else owe our very existence to God, the Creator. And he did not just create us like some divine watchmaker, setting everything ticking on its own so he could move on to other business. Indeed, not only the fact that we *came into being* but the fact that we and the universe are *sustained in being* and do not lapse back into nothingness is due to God's eternal power and love that uphold us. As St. Paul declared, it is through God that "we live and move and have our being," every day of our lives (Acts 17:28). *True humility, then, recognizes that we are creatures who depend upon God for our very existence.*

We owe the greatest debt of gratitude to God for the very fact that we came into existence, but God also crafted each one of us so that during our time here on earth we should grow: physically, intellectually, and spiritually. Humility plays a special role in fertilizing and nourishing such growth. Let's look at a few of the ways humility can act as a spiritual Miracle-Gro throughout the days and years of each of our lives on earth, literally from womb to tomb.

Humility Knows Its Limits: The Little Girl Who Failed Because She Thought She Didn't Need to Try

Intellectual humility and realistic self-awareness are not for great Church Doctors alone but for every one of us, with lessons to share throughout every stage of life. Consider the sad case of Sally, age five. Some psychologist has gotten a hold of her as a subject for an experiment on memory using what's called the Digit Span test. He tells Sally he is going to read her strings of numbers up to ten digits long and then ask her to call them back to him, in order. First, though, he asks Sally to guess how many numbers she thinks she can remember, and Sally tells him *all ten*! Next, the little experiment goes on, and how do you think Sally does? Well, she tops out not at ten digits, but four.

So where does humility fit in to this picture? Well, in some interesting little studies, children of various ages have indeed been asked to guess how many digits they would be able to recall before they took the test. Younger, especially preschool-age, children tend to *overestimate* their ability to recall information and are surprised to find that they cannot remember as much as they thought they could. (Indeed, one of my sons replicated this little experiment for a grade-school science project, and he found the same thing!) As children get older, their guesses about the powers of their own memory grow more and more accurate, most likely because their memories are actually put to the test in school and they get realistic feedback about what they and cannot do. This leads to what we might at least call a very realistic sense of "digit span humility."

But more than one important lesson on the power of humility comes from this simple experiment.

First of all, *humility entails a realistic assessment of our own skills* in whatever kind of endeavor we undertake. If we overestimate our capacities, we are likely to fail. After all, "pride goes before destruction, and a haughty spirit before a fall" (Proverbs 16:18). Granted, in the case of young children, their overestimated abilities are far more likely caused by ignorance than pride, but as we mature, *humility requires that we try to overcome ignorance of the limits of our capacities.* As we are advised in Scripture, "Seek not what is too difficult for you, nor investigate what is beyond your power" (Sirach 3:21) and, "Do not lift a weight beyond your strength" (Sirach 13:2).

Secondly, if we overestimate our abilities, we may well fail at tasks we *could have* accomplished. To get back to our simple digit span example, if Sally has no real sense of the limits of her memory abilities, she will fail to understand the need to focus and pay as close attention as possible when the numbers are called out or to repeat them quickly to herself, both of which enhance digit span performance. Believe it or not, St. Thomas Aquinas himself has specifically addressed human memory performance and improvement, and he designates concentration and repetition as two of four things we must do to maximize our natural memory abilities![27]

This should remind us that true humility is *realistic* and aimed at *truth*. It neither *overestimates* nor *underestimates* our true capacities in any area. Hopefully, as the years and the decades pile up throughout our own lives, we will pay close attention to both our growing powers, and the limits of those powers, so we will always try our best to reach goals that are realistic for us.

Humility Knows Its Powers Too: The Ambitious Boy Who "Spoke Papal"

Intellectual humility can also unlock our God-given powers throughout the entire life span. While Sirach warns us not to lift weights that are too heavy for us, every weight lifter knows that a weight that seems bone crushing when we first take up training can come to seem like child's play months or years down the road. *Having intellectual humility does not mean selling ourselves short*, as this next true story makes clear.

Once upon a time, within our own galaxy, more than ten years ago, a psychologist received a phone call from the mother of J.P., a ten-year-old boy with a rather unusual goal. He had read the psychologist's book on memory improvement and wanted to know how to memorize the names of every single pope, in order! Now, there were 265 of them at the time, and some had names like Zosimus and Eleutherius. Even for those with simpler names, like John, the boy would have to remember twenty-three of them, in their exact spots.

The psychologist, remembering that full natural memory capacities do not typically kick in until around age twelve or so, responded to the mother's call with advice on how to use special visual-imagery and location methods to see if the job could be done, and, though not wanting to be a doubting Thomas, cautioned her that it might exceed his capacities at this time and that he should not put undue pressure on himself if it seemed after a time that the task exceeded his limits.

A few months later, the psychologist heard an unfamiliar young voice on the phone that proceeded to tell him, "I did it!" Indeed, J.P. did learn how to recall and name all 265 popes!

Now, this is no fairy tale, since, as you may have guessed, I was the psychologist. My wife and I were invited to come see J.P. recite all the popes at a talent show within a convent. After J.P. had played the piano while his young brother sang a beautiful solo, he took center stage and named all the popes while his dad, standing behind him, pointed to each that he called off on a big laminated chart. J.P.'s grandfather told us he calls him "the boy who speaks papal."

Young J.P.'s story caught on. It was carried by the national Catholic News Agency. J.P., his mother, and I were even interviewed about it on a secular news station in New York. So what motivated J.P.? I would later find that his pastor, a former teacher, was an aficionado of memory techniques. Word got out that he had offered a monetary prize to any of his high school students who could memorize all the popes, but the prize remained unclaimed—until young J.P. came along! Coincidentally, a week prior to writing this, at a presentation in a different city of the same state, who should be there but that same parish priest. We reminisced about J.P.'s remarkable feat, and when I double-checked my memories of J.P. with Father (in front of a live audience) he confirmed that J.P. did indeed receive an "undisclosed" amount of money for his prodigious feat of papal memory!

Now, I am not naive enough to think that mastery of the names of all (now) 266 popes is on your bucket list either, but J.P. can teach us all that humility does *not* at all entail an "I cannot do it" mentality. As Sirach advises, do not seek what is too high for you, but do not hesitate to work on stretching your God-given powers to the max, to reach worthwhile goals that mean much to you.

Humility Learns Its New Growing Powers and Their Limits: A Teenage Samson Wannabe Gets a Haircut

As we pass from childhood into adolescence, we acquire a whole new array of physical and mental powers that we need to grow familiar with as we learn about our new capacities and new limitations, too.

Philosophers like Aristotle commented millennia ago (and lamented just a bit) about how adolescents tend to think and act. "They would always rather do noble deeds than useful ones: their lives are regulated more by their character than by reasoning ... All their mistakes are in the direction of doing things excessively and vehemently." They err "by overdoing everything; they love too much and hate too much, and the same with everything else."[28]

Modern developmental psychologists have extensively studied how various thinking abilities develop from infancy through childhood and adolescence. They note that in the early and mid teens, all kinds of abstract reasoning capacities are blossoming, including the capacity for hypothetical, if-then, reasoning.

Teens may become intoxicated with their newfound powers to hypothesize and think about personal and worldwide situations in new ways, and they may not hesitate to explain to older individuals (especially their parents) just how the world (or at least their household) should be run. They may build grand aims and noble plans to elevate humanity through their newfound wisdom, and yet, being young, they lack the experience to understand broader and deeper complicating factors that would reveal their utopian visions as ill-fitted pipe dreams.

Indeed, some of this is captured in the term "sophomore," for second-year high school (and college) students, deriving from the Greek *sophos* for wise and *moros* for fool! They are wise in terms of their new cognitive powers but perhaps a bit foolish because they haven't yet learned their limits.

Inebriated with these new mental powers, the adolescent tends to forget the fact that those powers were developed largely through what he or she learned from those older, more experienced, and wiser. Hopefully, as time goes by and their own experience accrues, adolescents may come to humbly appreciate once again the wisdom that comes with age.

A quote usually attributed to Mark Twain sums up the developmental sequence quite nicely: "When I was a boy of fourteen, my father was so ignorant I could hardly stand to have the old man around. But when I got to be twenty-one, I was astonished at how much the old man had learned in seven years." Perhaps, of course, it was *not* the "old man" who had done most of the learning! (Does this anecdote ring any personal bells from years gone by?)

Developmental psychologists have written extensively on what is called *adolescent egocentrism*, a rather distorted manner of thinking that results from the combination of new thinking powers that arise in adolescence with a lack of worldly experience, perhaps compounded as well by the significant, bewildering physical and emotional changes that occur after puberty.

In essence, adolescent thinking tends to be very *self*-conscious and *self*-centered. Noting that humility is sometimes described as *"not thinking less of ourselves but thinking of ourselves less,"*[29] these developmental tendencies are pretty diametrically opposed to the development of humility, though they may provide great fodder for growth in humility when we look back at how self-centered we were in those years (at least, that is the case for me!).

Psychologist David Elkind called two of the most famous elements of adolescent egocentrism the "personal fable" and the "imaginary audience," and believe me, I knew them both inside out as a teen. The *personal fable* refers to the tendency of adolescents to think they are unique and special. While in a sense each of us truly is unique and special, we are not any more unique or special than anyone else. This exaggerated sense of uniqueness can lead teens to think that no one (especially their parents) can truly understand them.

The personal fable can also lead to an unrealistic sense of the importance of one's potentials and the capacities of one's powers. If you were to ask, for example, a group of sixth graders who loved playing basketball on their school team for a show of hands from the ones who would one day play in the NBA, you would likely see many hands go up, regardless of the fact of how very few lovers of basketball, one in millions, are ever selected to play at that high level.

I confirmed this tendency myself in the 1990s when I did a study of adults going through a certification program to become fitness trainers with a specialization in bodybuilding methods. One question asked if they believed in their teens that they would become Mr. Olympia, holder of the number one title in the world of bodybuilding. Now, at the time there had been ten winners in history, and with a world population of close to three billion males, their odds were about 1 in 300 million. Yet the majority of respondents reported that they did, in their teenage years, think they would become the best bodybuilder in the world. Indeed, one man provided the greatest personal fable of all, having carved in the tree in his front yard his plan to win the Mr. Olympia title *ten times*! (As of this writing, none of us has won yet, and no one on earth has won more than eight times.)

Along these lines, allow me to confess that *I* am the "teenage Samson wannabe" of our section heading. I, too, thought at one time in my teens that I would become the greatest bodybuilder of all time! Then, as a seventeen-year-old in 1978, I attended a seminar with the first Mr. Universe ever to obtain a perfect score. He asked the audience if we would like to know the secret of becoming a world-class bodybuilder. Salivating like Pavlov's dogs, we waited for his words with bated breath, standing ready to lift weights for eight hours per day (or drink motor oil, if that's what it took). What a disappointment it was to hear his answer: "If you want to be a world-class bodybuilder, you must choose the right parents!" *Choose the right parents?! Now how were we going to do that?*

Mr. Universe had relayed to us a very humbling truth. It revealed his own humility, since he admitted that though he trained and dieted very seriously, his inherited genetic potential for things like naturally broad shoulders and narrow hips were indispensable ingredients for his own success. It was humbling for us to hear, since it meant that if we were blessed with more normal bodily features, we would likely never bear the title of Mr. Universe (even if we worked out all day for years and drank the highest-grade motor oil!).

Fortunately, a realistic sense of humility is a very good thing, even if Mr. Universe turned our personal fables into fractured fairy tales. After all, as he told us, though we might never become the best in the world, *we could always strive to become the best we can be given our own unique genetic potentials.* So while this would-be Samson got somewhat of a haircut that day, his locks would grow back, not to the length of a Samson, but to the right length for him, given the parents God gave him!

Another element of the personal fable can be a "sense of invincibility," leading youths to undertake very risky behaviors since a person of their unique destiny could not possibly die young. Now, those who see themselves as invulnerable to harm rarely spend much time humbly reflecting on their mortality and the fact that they are "ashes to ashes, dust to dust."

Then there is the imaginary audience. Many teens become so self-absorbed they assume that *others* are always focused on them too. This can lead to attention-seeking behaviors to satisfy their audience or to a heightened self-consciousness that makes teens easily embarrassed (as when peers see them out with their parents).

I recall this tendency well as my own natural shyness intensified in my teens. With a naturally ruddy complexion, I would flush and turn red at the slightest embarrassment. Indeed, I recall at times sitting in a high school classroom thinking to myself how embarrassing it would be *if* (that "if-then thinking" again!) I turned red right there for no reason and everyone noticed. Lo and behold, in seconds I would feel that hot flush in my cheeks. (Perhaps one of the greatest reliefs of growing a little older, wiser, and humbler is to cast aside the imaginary audience when we realize that most people are too busy focusing on their own lives to spend too much time focusing on ours.)

Speaking of focus, there is a sense in which both *wisdom* and *humility* themselves are matters of proper focus, of focusing on the things that matter the most. St. Thomas, paraphrasing Aristotle, wrote that "the slenderest knowledge that may be obtained of the highest things is more desirable than the most certain knowledge obtained of lesser things."[30] Knowledge of the highest things is *wisdom*, and the highest things are the things of God. Through *humility* we remove our focus from ourselves and place it upon God. In the words of St. Thomas: "But humility, considered as a special virtue, regards chiefly the subjection of man to God."[31]

Growing wiser with age, recognizing the limits of our powers and experience, growing less focused on ourselves and more focused on God—these are among the gifts that humility gives us, if we make the effort to unwrap them.

Humility Doesn't Pretend to Know What It Doesn't
(Said the Dolphin to the Monkey)

Back in the days of yore, upon the wine-dark seas near Athens, Greece, a ship full of men and one monkey was wrecked in the midst of a violent storm. As the crew hit the water, a pod of dolphins—mankind's friends—swam up to rescue them. One dolphin saw the monkey and, supposing him to be a man, let him perch on his back in order to save him. As they neared the Athenian shoreline, the dolphin asked him if he was an Athenian. The monkey responded that indeed he was, having descended from one of Athens' most important families. The dolphin proceeded to ask whether he knew Piraeus. The monkey replied that he knew "him" very well and in fact they were the closest of friends. Then the dolphin dove under the stormy sea and left the monkey to fend for himself.

It turns out that Piraeus was not a man, but a famous harbor near Athens, and the dolphin hated lies! This little tale is among the hundreds of Aesop's fables passed down to us from the famous sixth-century BC Greek fabulist, old Aesop himself. All are full of delightful moral lessons for children and, indeed, for adults too. The moral of this story involves the dangers of lying, but it also teaches a lesson of humility. Intellectual humility means knowing how much you don't know and being willing to learn from others, and it also means *not pretending to know what you don't know*. Perhaps if the monkey had the honesty and humility to admit he did not know Piraeus, the dolphin might well have landed him there high and dry.

Speaking not of monkeys and dolphins but of humans, someone once quipped along the same lines: "It is better to remain silent and be thought a fool than to open one's mouth and remove all doubt!" This quote is often attributed to Abraham Lincoln (my hometown of Springfield, Illinois' greatest son—if you will pardon the boast!) was not only self-taught in law but was literally well versed in Scripture too. He would have known well the words of Proverbs 17:28: "Even a fool who keeps silent is considered wise; when he closes his lips, he is deemed intelligent."

Indeed, the Old Testament book of Proverbs is replete with comparisons and contrasts between the characteristics and behaviors of people who act foolishly, compared to those who act wisely. Let's look at a quick sample:

Folly Versus Wisdom
in the Book of Proverbs

The fool ...	The wise person ...
"rejects reproof" and "goes astray" (Proverbs 10:17)	loves you when you reprove him; grows wiser from instruction (Proverbs 9:8–9)
"is right in his own eyes" (Proverbs 12:15)	"listens to advice" (Proverbs 12:15)
"throws off restraint and is careless" (Proverbs 14:16)	"is cautious and turns away from evil" (Proverbs 14:16)
"has a hasty temper" (Proverbs 14:29)	"is slow to anger" (Proverbs 14:29)
"gives full vent to his anger" (Proverbs 29:11)	"quietly holds it back" (Proverbs 29:11)
has eyes "on the ends of the earth" (Proverbs 17:24)	"sets his face toward wisdom" (Proverbs 17:24)
"takes no pleasure in understanding, but only in expressing his opinion" (Proverbs 18:2)	finds "wise conduct" a "pleasure" (Proverbs 10:23)
"will be quarreling" (Proverbs 20:3)	attains honor in keeping "aloof from strife" (Proverbs 20:3)
repeats his foolishness, "like a dog that returns to his vomit" (Proverbs 26:11)	will "lay up knowledge" (Proverbs 10:14)

Do you detect any connections between *a lack of humility* and *foolishness* and between *humility* and *wisdom*? Humility may be the "new smart," but it's always been the "old smart" too! Let's also highlight the words "knowledge," "understanding," and "wisdom" in those verses, for they are indeed the three intellectual virtues (and gifts of the Holy Spirit) that humility sets free, as we will see in our next story.

Humility Leads to Wisdom: The Elderly Professor Who Wanted to Know "Everything!"

"That means I want to know *everything*!" That's what the man said. You see, when I went through my psychology doctoral program in the early 1990s, one of my most delightful and inspiring professors was a man who completed his doctorate while in his sixties. After a successful career in business, he pursued wholeheartedly his burning desire to learn about the workings of the human mind. He told the class one day that his desire was actually to become a "polymath," which he said with a gleam in his eye (and tongue partially in cheek), meaning that he wanted to know *"everything*!"

I really admired him for that, especially since, as a first-year doctoral student, it seemed I still had everything *left* to learn! Of course, we obviously don't have the time or capacity to learn everything. We must set some priorities. After all, some things are far more worth knowing than others. Perhaps loftier than the goal to learn about everything is the goal to *learn everything we can about lofty things*. This is why, modifying a bit my professor's example, I like to think to myself now, "I don't want to know everything—just everything *worth knowing*."

Well, the desire to pursue what is truly worth knowing is but one of many aspects of the intellectual virtue of *wisdom*. The fact that wisdom recognizes we cannot know everything already shows how it rests upon a foundation of *intellectual humility*. So, let's take a quick peek at the "intellectual virtues" according to the words of Scripture, and of St. Thomas Aquinas.

Humility Holds Up a Holy House

"By wisdom a house is built, and by understanding it is established; by knowledge the rooms are filled with all precious and pleasant riches" *(Proverbs 24:3–4).*

Not only does humility serve as the sturdy foundation of a temple housing all of the virtues, it also solidly grounds a holy and mighty house! Our verse from Proverbs names three lofty intellectual virtues (and, as we will see later in this chapter, three yet loftier gifts of the Holy Spirit)— namely, wisdom, understanding, and knowledge.

To put their nature as virtues in three nutshells, St. Thomas tells us that *understanding* denotes our capacity to grasp underlying principles and natures of things through abstract, conceptual thinking; *knowledge* (also called "science," from Latin *scire,* "to know") denotes the capacity to grasp cause-and-effect relationships through observation and chains of reasoning; while *wisdom,* the highest of them all, distinguishes itself "by judging both of the conclusions of science, and of the principles on which they are based."[32] It is through understanding and knowledge that we grasp the facts of reality and through wisdom that we grasp the highest and most important realities of all. Now, the house of all three of these wonderful, uniquely human capacities also stands firmly upon a foundation of humility. So let's see how.

The Man Deemed Wise Because He Knew There Was So Much He Didn't Know

The most famous story of the search for truth and wisdom in classical literature is that of the humble founder of Western philosophy, Socrates (c. 470–399 BC). Plato wrote that when the Oracle of Delphi declared Socrates the wisest man in Athens, Socrates was shocked, trusting the oracle's veracity but knowing he himself was not wise. He then went around interviewing prominent men to find someone wiser than he. He found, to his dismay, that each great man was quick to sing the praises of his own wisdom. Socrates was not impressed. Finally, it occurred to him that his unique wisdom consisted in knowing that he knew so little. He did not pretend to know things that he didn't know, and he always went around questioning others as he sought out the truth. Socrates knew how to put intellectual humility into the service of wisdom!

Indeed, Socrates grasped the wisdom of the precepts St. Frances de Sales would lay out for Christians centuries later: "To think one knows what he does not know is an evident stupidity; to wish to appear learned about a subject of which one knows that he is actually ignorant is a display of insupportable vanity."[33]

We don't see much when our eyes are closed, and neither do we understand much when our minds are closed because we see no need to open them, sometimes even before we open our mouths. Remember how "a fool takes no pleasure in understanding, but only in expressing his opinion" (Proverbs 18:2)? Hmm … had good King Solomon foreseen social media posting three millennia before its time? Seriously, we are in no position to penetrate into the heart of the truth of any matter if we believe we already know it all—and can't wait to let others know just how well we know it.

Intellectual humility equips us with the recognition that there may well be much more to know about things that we think we already grasp, and it opens us up to further truths and deeper levels of understanding. Further, excepting issues of dogmas of faith revealed by God and set forth by the Church, humility reminds us that what we may think we understand about various matters may be very incomplete, or even flat-out wrong.

Indeed, humility acknowledges both the humor and the truth of a popular aphorism: "It ain't so much the things we don't know that get us into trouble. It's the things we know that ain't so."[34]

Sadly, in our modern information age we are constantly bombarded by worldly wisdom from every perspective from countless electronic news and social media outlets. It seems that almost everyone has an opinion on every important topic and stands more than ready to share their questionable wisdom with others. (And woe to those who might disagree!)

Indeed, we should be aware that the computerized algorithms of the Internet and social media constantly monitor our online behavior to increase our time online and maximize the profits to advertisers and

Internet companies. This is done in such a way that particular news items and articles that match our views and interests are selectively presented to us, catering to how each of us sees our own "truth" and filtering out opposing views. No wonder we see so much polarization and lack of humility and respect for the views of others in our time. Oh, for a self-doubting Socrates now and then![35]

Humility and wisdom go hand in hand, and when one of the two is missing, the other is nowhere to be found.

Humility Asks God for the Wisdom from Above (and the Other Six Gifts)

As valuable as human wisdom can be, Scripture also teaches us there is a "wisdom from above" which is "first pure, then peaceable, gentle, open to reason, full of mercy and good fruits, without uncertainty or insincerity" (James 3:17). And how do we obtain it? James tells us quite clearly: "If any of you lacks wisdom, let him ask God, who gives to all men generously and without reproaching, and it will be given him" (James 1:5).

When it comes to perfection of our intellectual powers, despite the excellence of the natural virtues of science, understanding, and wisdom, God isn't nearly finished with us yet. If we humble our minds and hearts before him, he will gladly help us know more, understand more deeply, and live our lives far more wisely then we ever could on our own. You see, wisdom is also among the seven gifts of the Holy Spirit, which, along with the gifts of knowledge and understanding, perfect our human virtues of the same names.

The *virtues* are perfections of our powers that operate by bringing our thoughts, emotions, and actions under the guidance of *right reason*, our highest, though fallible, natural guide to the true and the good. God has also made available to us seven *gifts* of the Holy Spirit that can guide our thoughts, feeling, and behaviors not merely by human reason but by the infallible inspiration of the Holy Spirit himself. The virtues have been described as oars on a boat that we use to row ourselves toward noble goals, while the gifts of the Holy Spirit are like massive sails that allow the wind of the Holy Spirit to carry us quickly toward godly goals on earth, and ultimately toward eternal bliss with God in heaven. Here they are as they appear in the Bible:

> There shall come forth a shoot from the stump of Jesse,
>   and a branch shall grow out of his roots.
> And the Spirit of the LORD shall rest upon him,
>   the spirit of wisdom and understanding,
>   the spirit of counsel and might,
>   the spirit of knowledge and the fear of the LORD.
> And his delight shall be in the fear of the LORD. (Isaiah 11:1–3)

Isaiah is prophesying about the coming of Jesus Christ, who will receive the Holy Spirit's gifts in their fullest measure, but the Church teaches that we *all* receive them in Baptism and have them strengthened (made firm) in Confirmation.

As the *Catechism of the Catholic Church* states, "The seven gifts of the Holy Spirit bestowed upon Christians are wisdom, understanding, counsel, fortitude, knowledge, piety, and fear of the Lord" (CCC 1845). (Since you may wonder where *piety* came from, given the translation of Isaiah provided above, I'll mention that in St. Jerome's Vulgate translation of the Bible in Latin, from which the Catholic teaching arose, verse two ends with *"pietatis"* [piety], and *"timoris Domini"* [fear of the Lord] comes only at the end.)

Medieval theologians noted that there is a ranking of sorts among the gifts. They said Isaiah describes them from the highest (wisdom) down to the lowest (fear of the Lord) *as they descend from the Holy Spirit upon man.* And yet, *if we arrange them in reverse order, they form a spiritual ladder* on which we take the first step through fear of the Lord. Eventually, having moved up the seven steps of the ladder, "there opens to us at the end of the ascent the entrance to the life of Heaven."[36] We see this progression suggested several times in Scripture where fear of the Lord is described as "the beginning of wisdom" (Psalm 111:10; Proverbs 9:10 and 15:33; Sirach 1:14). Let's lay this out schematically and take a good look at it.

The Descent and Ascension of the Holy Spirit's Gifts

Descent from the **Holy Spirit** to Man
(order of description in Isaiah 11:2–3)

Loving Union **with God** at the Apex
(per St. Gregory the Great and St. Robert Bellarmine)

WISDOM	WISDOM
UNDERSTANDING	UNDERSTANDING
COUNSEL	COUNSEL
FORTITUDE	FORTITUDE
KNOWLEDGE	KNOWLEDGE
PIETY	PIETY
FEAR of the LORD	FEAR of the LORD

Grounded in Humility

Man's Supernatural Stairway to Heaven

As I have written elsewhere, for that first step of fear of the Lord, seventeenth-century Dominican theologian John of St. Thomas tells us that *humility* is different from *fear*, as Our Lord showed us when he humbly washed the disciples' feet—while he certainly did not fear them. Nevertheless, "humility can flow from fear and be regulated by it,"[37] and St. Thomas said that humility can be an *effect* of fear. If we fear God perfectly, we will humbly acknowledge that we are nothing apart from him, the Creator and the One who keeps everything in existence. St. Catherine of Siena knew this, as she heard God say to her, "Do you know, daughter, who you are, and who I am? If you know these two things you will be blessed. You are she who is not; whereas I am He who is."[38]

While humility can flow from fear of the Lord, be regulated by it, and be its effect, *there is also a sense in which humility can open our hearts and minds to all of the Holy Spirit's gifts.* Those imbued with pride may believe they can row themselves to heaven, without the aid of God's grace, while it takes humility to admit we cannot get there on our own and to be willing to get down on our knees and pray, to unfurl our sails so we may be taken wherever the Holy Spirit leads us.

As for our three intellectual *gifts*, and how they perfect and complete the intellectual *virtues*, please allow the Angelic Doctor to briefly unwrap them:

- "Knowledge of human things is called 'knowledge,'" and regarding matters of faith, "to know what one ought to believe, belongs to the gift of knowledge."[39]

- "Man needs a supernatural light in order to penetrate further still so as to know what it cannot know by its natural light: and this supernatural light which is bestowed on man is called the gift of understanding.[40]

- "The knowledge of Divine things may be properly called wisdom," and regarding matters of faith, "to know [them] in themselves ... by a kind of union with them, belongs to the gift of wisdom."[41] "Wisdom as a gift is more excellent than wisdom as an intellectual virtue, since it attains to God more intimately by a kind of union of the soul with Him, it is able to direct us not only in contemplation but also in action."[42]

Another wonderful fact about even the loftiest of the gifts of the Holy Spirit is that God is so willing to grace us with them—if we are simply humble enough to ask him. Remember: "If any of you lacks wisdom, let him ask God, who gives to all men generously and without reproaching, and it will be given him" (James 1:5).

We will conclude here with one last point about the *sweet joy* humility can bring us when it opens us to the highest spiritual gifts that perfect our minds. We saw that *sophia* is the Greek word for wisdom. The Latin word for wisdom is *sapientia.* Let's listen to St. Thomas' last words of wisdom, for now: "Augustine is speaking of wisdom as to its cause, whence also wisdom [*sapientia*] takes its name, in so far as it denotes a certain sweetness [*saporem*]." Indeed, "wisdom [*sapientia*] may be described as 'sweet-tasting science [*sapida scientia*].'" What could possibly be sweeter than "a kind of union of the soul with Him" brought about through the Holy Spirit's gift of wisdom?[43] In the words of King David: "O taste and see that the LORD is good!" (Psalm 34:8).

How fitting that a lifetime spent humbly seeking the truth of the Lord will provide us such sweet everlasting rewards.

Humility's Holy Toolbox:

Intellectual Humility and the Virtues of Learning

1. **Pray for *intellectual humility* and the wisdom from above.** Here, for example, is a brief excerpt of some of St. Thomas' own words when he prayed for humility within his prayer "To Acquire the Virtues":

   Lord, "grant that I may always observe modesty in the way I dress, the way I walk, and the gestures I use ... lower my gaze in humility, lift my mind to thoughts of heaven, contemn all that will pass away, and love You only."[44]

   And here are words from his prayers for intellectual virtues and gifts from his prayer "Before Study":

   Lord, "grant to me keenness of mind, capacity to remember, skill in learning, subtlety to interpret, and eloquence in speech. May You guide the beginning of my work, direct its progress, and bring it to completion."[45]

2. **Embrace and honor the sacrament of Holy Orders.** The Church Fathers and Doctors paired the four cardinal virtues (which we will see in chapter 2) and the three theological virtues (the stuff of our chapter 3) to each of the seven sacraments. Indeed, we will learn of all of these pairings in the pages ahead. Though they did not single out the intellectual virtues of understanding, knowledge, and wisdom, they associated the sacrament of Holy Orders with a special kind of wisdom that is directed toward the

practical actions we make in our daily lives. It is called *practical wisdom* or *prudence*, as we will see in more depth in our next chapter.

Those whom God calls to Holy Orders act as Christ for us on earth and bring us his special graces through the sacraments. They go through specialized training to grow in holiness and to grow in deep knowledge, understanding, and wisdom about our Faith, so that they may also serve as our spiritual guides to help us grow in humility, wisdom, and holiness.

A simple way we can exercise our humility when we interact with men who have received Holy Orders is to call them by their titles—"Deacon" or "Father," "Your Excellency" for bishops and archbishops, and "Your Eminence" for a cardinal. Of course, we should say "Your Holiness" or "Most Holy Father" when directly addressing the pope.

Further, though some men in religious orders also have received Holy Orders, there are many monks who have not, whom we commonly respectfully refer to as "Brother." As for religious sisters, addressing them as "Sister" should be music to their ears, and if they happen to hold an office with a title like "Reverend Mother," we also honor them and humble ourselves by addressing them with their hard-earned—and God-given—titles.

May they all help guide us toward heaven!

Chapter 1 Summary and Reflections

Humility aids us in gaining a deeper understanding of the reality of ourselves in our nature, our place in the universe, and in our utter dependence on God who created and sustains us. By exercising the *intellectual humility* that shows gratitude to God for giving us intellectual capacities of *knowledge, understanding,* and *wisdom* unique among all creatures on earth, we stand willing to acknowledge the limits of our own knowledge and seek out earthly and heavenly teachers from whom we may learn—and above all by heeding Christ's call to learn from him while remaining open to the stirrings of the Holy Spirit.

We would do well to examine our consciences at the end of the day and ask ourselves which of our thoughts and actions fostered growth in intellectual humility and intellectual virtues and which have hindered them. (I'll put them in the singular for you—and me.)

- Have I sought to hear both sides and "penetrate to the heart" of complicated issues, or have I kept my eyes and mind closed since I am sure I know all I need to know already?

- Have I used my intellectual powers to row my boat toward truth, or have I let them lie dormant in their oarlocks?

- Have I thanked God for the inborn dispositions to acquire humility and intellectual virtues and done what I can so that those dispositions grow into virtues as a child matures into an adult?

- Have I shown the humility to unfurl my sails to move with the winds of the Holy Spirit or have I decided I can do it on my own?

- Have I read the Bible today for lessons of humility and all of the intellectual virtues it undergirds after praying for the Holy Spirit's guidance, or have I left its pages unopened or, through haste or inattention, left the heart of its lessons unpenetrated?

- Have I prayed today to God for humility and wisdom?

- Have I honored the men ordained in Holy Orders and sought to grow in my understanding and knowledge of the key teachings of the Church?

Humility Lived Saint Story #1:

St. Albert the Great, Patron Saint of Scientists

I recommend to you particularly the virtues of courage, which defends science in a world marked by doubt, alienated from truth, and in need of meaning; and humility, through which we recognize the finiteness of reason before Truth which transcends it. These are the virtues of Albert the Great.[46]

—St. John Paul II

Albert of Cologne (c.1200–1280) was known as Albert "the Great" even while he was alive, and yet, as John Paul II tells us, he was a saintly model of humility (not to mention the intellectual virtues and gifts). He was called great because of his mastery not only of theology and philosophy but of the natural sciences, having written profound books on almost every science you could name, from astronomy, through botany and biology, geology, and geography, all the way to zoology. This is why the Church has honored him with the title of the "Universal Doctor" and designated him the patron saint of scientists.

Albert's humility rang out loud and clear in his books on the natural sciences because he studied creation to learn about (and teach us about) the glories of its Creator. He studied effects to learn about their ultimate Cause: "The first [cause], God—the most true, most sweet, most powerful from eternity forever and ever and reigning through boundless ages—can be known in another way, that is, through his effects."[47] Further, "the whole world is theology for us, because the heavens proclaim the glory of God."[48]

Albert, was, in his prime, the most respected theologian and professor in the world. Yet, as a Dominican preacher, teacher, and commentator on Scripture, he was well aware of St. Paul's advice to "count others better than yourselves" (Philippians 2:3), which he gladly did. Despite all his humble greatness, Albert is probably best known today as the teacher of a man whose intellectual achievements eclipsed even those of his own, St. Thomas Aquinas. A famous early story recalls that when fellow students nicknamed the large, lumbering, quiet Thomas "the dumb ox," Albert, who recognized his student's rare abilities, informed the whole class that one day the bellowing of that ox would be heard around the world! Indeed, it was heard even during Thomas' and Albert's own lifetimes and reverberates in our own time.

A lesser-known anecdote displaying humility in action occurred in 1277, three years after Albert experienced the unexpected death of his most remarkable and saintly student. Bishop Tempier of Paris had deemed a series of 219 modern philosophical and theological theses "heretical," and the list included a number of propositions that were consistent with St. Thomas' teachings. Now, bear in mind that John Paul said not only *humility* but *courage* were the virtues of St. Albert. The aging Albert walked about 250 miles to Paris to publicly defend each and every one of St. Thomas' theses. He returned to Cologne and pored over in sequence all the voluminous works of his late student and friend. He was so awed by Thomas' *Summa Theologica* that he ceased writing his own and tirelessly championed St. Thomas' work within the Dominican Order and throughout the Church. When most others would prioritize their own work and notoriety, St. Albert championed that of another. Clearly the "great" one was also a "humble" one. Indeed, he would speak and write ardently on behalf of St. Thomas, saying that "by his writings [he] laboured for all to the end of the world, and that henceforth all others would work in vain."[49]

St. Albert, pray for us, that we might know true greatness lies in humility and courage, that every effect might remind us of its ultimate Cause, that our humility and courage might bolster others, and that we may never forget that "from the greatness and beauty of created things comes a corresponding perception of their Creator" (Wisdom 13:5).[50]

Chapter 2

HUMILITY DOES GOOD

*Who is wise and understanding among you? By his good life
let him show his works in the meekness of wisdom.*

—James 3:13

As we move from the intellectual virtues, the "virtues of learning," to the moral virtues, the "virtues of living," our focus will move from discerning what is *true* to achieving what is *good,* to using that knowledge to act in the world, doing good works while displaying a gentle humility.

Two Forms of Goodness/Four Cardinal Virtues

Aristotle noted long ago that "goodness has two forms, moral virtue and intellectual excellence; for we praise not only the just but also the intelligent and the wise."[51] We have addressed the intellectual virtues of the wise, including wisdom itself. Now we consider the virtues that make a person not only wise, but *just,* if *humility* undergirds them.

St. Thomas writes that "for a man to do a good deed, it is requisite not only that his reason be well disposed by means of a habit of intellectual virtue; but also that his appetite be well disposed by means of a habit of moral virtue."[52] St. James knew well that true wisdom is displayed in one's works, when the actions of one's daily life are marked by *prauteti* in the Greek, translated as "meekness" or "gentleness," and sometimes as "humility" itself.

Now, in both the writings of the best of pagan philosophy and in the Holy Scriptures, *four* particular moral virtues have been understood to capture the essence of moral virtue. We have already hinted at two of them in this chapter: justice, drawing from Aristotle's statement on "the just," and prudence, or *practical wisdom* lived out in daily life, drawing from the verse of St. James. These and two others have been known for millennia, as we noted in the beginning of part 1, as the cardinal virtues, deriving from the Latin word *cardo* for hinge.

Here are all four in the same verse in the Bible: "And if any one loves righteousness, her labors are virtues; for she teaches self-control and prudence, justice and courage" (Wisdom 8:7). Bearing in mind that self-control is a synonym for the virtue of temperance, we can see that these four "cardinals" have long been praised, endorsed, and labored at by any who would be righteous.

The Four Cardinal Virtues
per St. Thomas Aquinas

Virtues	Human powers they perfect
Temperance	Concupiscible appetite (passion to seek what we desire as good)
Fortitude	Irascible appetite (passion to overcome or endure obstacles to our good)
Justice	Will (aka "intellectual appetite": seeks to obtain good things, overcome/ endure bad things as judged not by passion but through right reason)
Prudence	Practical intellect (use of reason to determine moral means to attain moral goals)

What do these high-flying cardinals have to do with lowly humility? St. Thomas has shown that humility aids in the flight of all four of them, not to mention the host of *other associated virtues* that soar along with those cardinals. Indeed, he often called those associated virtues "parts" of the cardinal virtues, and we will need all of those parts to completely assemble humility in our souls. We must also bear in mind that these high-flying virtues are always ready to swoop down to assist us in even the most seemingly mundane tasks of our daily lives. So let's take a look at how these cardinals fly down to our aid in response to humility's bird call.

How Humility Overcomes Fears: The Youth Who Harnessed Humility to Defeat What Three Out of Four of Us Fear

There are so many things of which we can be afraid. I just did a simple Internet search for "most common fears" that yielded one article with a list of ninety-nine fears (maybe a hundred if I miscounted) that have acquired fancy clinical names from ancient Greek. You probably know several of them and, like me, might share a few, such as acrophobia (fear of heights), arachnophobia (fear of spiders), or ophidiophobia (fear of snakes).

In some people, fears like these can be so extreme that they seriously impair daily functioning and require some form of psychological therapy. The National Institute of Mental Health estimates that about 12.5 percent of Americans fall into this category at some point in their lives,[53] but those folks, and the other 87.5 percent of us, will also likely experience *some* degree of fear about all kinds of things we encounter in our daily lives, especially fears that arise in *social situations*. Would you believe that one of the greatest cures for social fears—fears that other people might ignore, reject, ridicule, or persecute us—is humility? How so? Let me explain.

Be Not Afraid!

I imagine most readers will recall that St. John Paul II was famous for his oft-repeated encouraging admonition "Be not afraid!" Of course, he was echoing Scripture, where this message appears hundreds of times, as when Jesus told his disciples: "Let not your hearts be troubled, neither let them be afraid" (John 14:27). Christ overcame all of the fears of his human nature, and he bid us to be like him in humility. So please allow me to humble myself by showing how humility helped me overcome one of my own greatest fears (though I would not actually realize it was humility that had helped me conquer that fear until a couple of decades after the event!).

When I was young I shared a very common fear, one known firsthand by so many in the way it can make your heart pound, your cheeks flush, your hands sweat, and your voice quiver—the dreaded *glossophobia*. Recent data shows about seventy-seven percent of people report they have this *fear of public speaking*. Of a naturally ruddy complexion and shy temperament, I would blush scarlet red and feel my heart begin to pound as beads of sweat would form even at the thought of having to speak before others, usually in a class at school. If a teacher assigned some kind of speech at the end of a course, I would wonder about the odds that he or she might get ill by the end of the term so I would be off the hook.

Later, thanks be to God, people who knew me well were astounded that I would go on to teach dozens of college courses and to give many dozens of public talks fearlessly without a written note. So how did this come to be?

Well, in my senior year of college, I was required to give a talk in front of one of my psychology classes. Fortunately, I had been studying techniques of cognitive therapy that can help one overcome negative emotions, including exaggerated fears. One technique has been called "negative visualization" by modern psychologists and *premeditatio malorum* by ancient Stoic philosophers. Here, you basically imagine the worst possible outcome of an upcoming situation you fear and train yourself to remain calm about it.

Borrowing from the insights of modern cognitive therapists, *before* I gave the talk I thought to myself something like this: "Suppose I get up there and turn red as a tomato, my voice falters, I crack a joke and nobody laughs, forget what I want to say next, accidentally spit on the people in the front row, and then look down to see that my shoes don't match and my zipper is open. Well, I might well be the worst public speaker in the world, but I suppose somebody has to be—so it might as well be me! I still have to do this talk to get my grade, so full steam ahead anyway!"

There is a second technique I used as I actually *began* the talk. It too has a name in modern cognitive therapy, namely "shame-attacking exercises," and roots in ancient Stoic philosophy. Modern psychologist Albert Ellis, treating patients in New York City, would advise people fearful of what others thought of them to go out and do things like walking a banana on a leash like a dog or standing backwards in a crowded elevator, so they would see that even if people did notice them and think them odd, it's not a devastating thing.[54]

An ancient form of this method was used on Zeno of Citium, founder of Stoic philosophy, by his teacher Crates. Crates realized that Zeno was too shy and concerned with what others thought about him, so he had him join him on a jaunt around Athens while carrying a huge crock of lentil soup. Zeno tried to hide the crock with his cloak out of embarrassment when some people walked by, so Crates took his staff and smashed open the crock, spilling bean soup all over Zeno's legs. When young Zeno ran off in shame, Crates called out, "Why run away, my little Phoenician... nothing terrible has befallen you."[55]

So here's what I did to attack my own shame when I had to give that talk. I brought no banana or lentil soup, but I merely apologized in advance to the class if they could see me flush and sweat and hear my heart pounding within my chest as I spoke. In essence, I made my fear that people would notice the physical signs of my extreme nervousness come true, and then I got on with the talk with a lot less redness, sweat, and tachycardia than ever before. To this day I can give talks without any excessive jitters.

I did not recognize for decades that *humility* played a huge role in overcoming my fear of public speaking, because I was far from true humility and far from the Church at the time, being in the early years of a twenty-five-year wilderness of atheism before the stirrings of the Holy Spirit and the words of Aquinas' *Summa Theologica* drew me back to God and the Church in my early forties. Still, those psychological and philosophical tools I employed indeed brought the *natural* virtue of humility into play, *whether I realized it or not*.

As we have noted, some say that humility is "not thinking less of ourselves but thinking of ourselves less," and that is precisely what such techniques help us do. Modern psychology speaks of approaching tasks from either an "ego orientation," where one focuses on oneself and how one will be perceived in comparison to others or from a "task orientation," where one focuses not on oneself and how one will be received but on competent performance of the task itself.

The Greco-Roman Stoic philosopher Epictetus (c. AD 50–135) brought this idea up more than once precisely when addressing public speaking and other public performances. He said some speakers are highly knowledgeable and fluent when conversing with friends yet become all tongue-tied when they speak before a live audience, just as some musicians display mastery of their instrument when playing by themselves but falter before an audience.[56] The reason is that their focus when in public is on how other people will evaluate them, praise them, or criticize them rather than on their talk's subject matter or the music itself.

When we cultivate humility, this can free us from our fear of failure and enhance our ability to do well in any worthwhile task we choose to pursue because *humility helps us focus on the task before us without worrying about propping up our own fragile egos.*

Natural humility says, "I will do my best at the task at hand to provide the maximum possible benefit to others, but if I should fail, oh well, I'll put my nose back to the grindstone and try, try again."

Christian humility declares with infinitely more power, "I might well fail this time, being but 'ashes to ashes, dust to dust,' but I will get up to work harder and try again, not forgetting that in the long run 'I can do all things in him who strengthens me' (Philippians 4:13)."

Indeed, if our task should involve speaking important truths of the Faith, we might remember as well what Christ told his friends: "Do not be anxious about how or what you are to answer or what you are to say; for the Holy Spirit will teach you in that very hour what you ought to say" (Luke 12:11–12).

How Humility Fortifies Fortitude

At this point, we have seen how humility helps undergird and even fortify the virtue of courage or fortitude when it comes to dealing with social fears. When we are not inordinately concerned with ourselves, with our own reputation or safety, we are in the best position to remain strong and courageous.

Fortitude comes from the Latin *fortis*, for "strong," and the most common synonym for this cardinal virtue is courage. Fortitude serves to bring our emotions and passions under the guidance of reason, but St. Thomas Aquinas tells us its special role is to moderate *fear* and *daring*. Fortitude serves to rein in our fear, so we can withstand or "bear the assault" of difficult obstacles, and it can also serve to bolster us to overcome some difficulties and "to dispel them altogether."[57] We can best "bear assaults" when we are not always focused on protecting our own egos. We can best dare to "overcome" obstacles and difficulty when our focus is on the good things we are striving to obtain rather than on the hardships they may pose to us.

Fortitude is one of the four crucial cardinal virtues, the "virtues of living," as we are calling them here. I mentioned that this book will address the parts we need to grow in humility and virtue, so let's quickly address the "parts" of fortitude. St. Thomas said fortitude's role has two aspects: first, the positive capacity to *overcome obstacles*, and second, the negative capacity to *endure hardships*. Here is how Thomas laid out the four virtues that help flesh out the fullness of the virtue of fortitude:

Fortitude and Its Four "Parts"

Overcoming Parts (Virtues)	Enduring Parts (Virtues)
Magnanimity	Patience
Magnificence	Perseverance

We will consider all four of these "parts" and how they relate to humility, but we'll zoom in the most on one part that some people have said may actually *oppose* humility.

Men of Magnanimity Multiply Their Talents

St. Thomas has noted that *magnanimity* has sometimes been thought to oppose the virtue of humility. Let's check this out in some depth and see how St. Thomas dissolves this virtuous paradox.

One issue St. Thomas Aquinas turns to again and again is humility's relationship to the virtue of magnanimity, whose name we can translate as greatness of soul, deriving from the Latin *magnus* for "great" and *animus* for "soul." Per Thomas, "magnanimity by its very name denotes stretching forth of the mind to great things."[58] Some in Thomas' day thought that magnanimity, having been written about most extensively by the pagan Aristotle (under the Greek word *megalopsyche*, also meaning greatness of soul), was incompatible with Christian humility and, indeed, more akin to the *sin* of pride. Aristotle wrote, for example, that the great-souled man walks slowly and talks with a deep, calm voice. He focuses on great things, and he scarcely needs anything. This might suggest to some that the great-souled man walks with his nose in the air, disdaining even the scent of those with smaller souls!

Thomas, however, championed magnanimity as a virtue to be pursued by every follower of Christ. Indeed, he saw one of Jesus' parables as a praising the Christian greatness of soul—the parable of the talents in Matthew 25:14–30. Before going on a journey, a wealthy man calls together three servants and gives each of them a sum of money "to each according to his ability" (Matthew 25:15). He gives one servant five "talents," another servant two talents, and a third servant one talent. Now, even one talent was of considerable worth, the equivalent of about *fifteen years'* wages of a laborer.

Do you recall what the master found upon his return? The man entrusted with five talents worked with them. He traded with them and produced five more for his master. The man with two did likewise, presenting his master with four talents when he came home. The master was quite pleased, of course. He told them how happy he was that they had been so faithful in caring for "a little," and that he would set them over "much" (Matthew 25:23).

But what about the third servant? Why did his actions with the talent entrusted to him so raise the ire of his master? Had he squandered the money on wine, women, and song? No, he had not. Had he gambled it away? By no means. In fact, he returned to the master the very same talent he had been given, after he had unearthed it from the hole in the ground that he had dug for its successful safekeeping.

And how exactly did the master react? He took that talent from the servant and gave it to the man who had ten—"For to every one who has will more be given, and he will have abundance; but from him who has not, even what he has will be taken away. And cast the worthless servant into the outer darkness, where there will be weeping and gnashing of teeth" (Matthew 25:29–30).

This story may seem harsh on its surface. Did the third servant perhaps exercise humility, playing it safe with the talent his master gave him because he knew he lacked the capabilities of the other two servants? Further, isn't there much more to virtue than money?

Well, this parable relates far more than a tale of a master and his servants, of course. It tells the story of our relationship to God, to the "talents" he has given us, and to our rewards, both here on earth right now and later in the eternal heavenly kingdom. The talents, of course, stand for much more than money. They represent all the good things God has given us— and our call to make the most of them.

So why was the master so angry with the man who had buried his under the ground? It was certainly not because he did not give him as many new talents as the other two servants. The master knew the men's varying capacities to begin with and was as pleased with the servant who returned four talents as with the servant who gave him back ten. He would certainly have been equally pleased if the third servant had given him back merely two. The problem was that God gives us all varying abilities and capacities, and he expects us to take them, run with them, multiply them, do good for others with them, and glorify him thereby. It is through magnanimity, or greatness of soul, that we strive to enhance our talents and do great things commensurate with our own abilities.

Indeed, the third servant who buried his talent underground displayed not humility but the vice that truly opposes greatness of soul, namely, smallness of soul—*pusillanimity*, which derives from the Latin word *pusillus*, meaning very little, petty, or paltry.

"Pusillanimity makes a man fall short of what is proportionate to his power ... Hence it is that the servant who buried in the earth the money he had received from his master, and did not trade with it through fainthearted fear, was punished by his master."[59]

Clearly then, Jesus himself, teller of the parable, would have us be great-souled, using our powers, investing them for the benefit of neighbor and the glory of God. We should strive for magnanimity in ourselves and in those under our charge, from as early an age as possible.

Humility and Magnanimity in Action: The Man Who Did Not Know What He Should Do with His Life (and the Man Who Swiftly Told Him)

Let's consider a true story of humility and magnanimity in more modern times. A young man heard that a world-renowned psychiatrist, a former associate of Sigmund Freud, would be speaking in his town. He attended the lecture and cornered the great man after his talk to ask him one "simple" question. He explained that he could not decide what kind of career to pursue. He had spent the last several years doing extensive research on a variety of fields and had examined the course offerings of dozens of universities, yet he was no closer to making up his mind than he was when he started. Could the learned psychiatrist advise him on how to proceed? The psychiatrist, who had never met the man before, instantly replied that he could indeed tell him which career he ought to pursue! (Do we detect, perhaps, a *lack* of humility here?)

He told the young man that since he had spent so much time and energy investigating all sorts of possible career choices that he should become *a career guidance counselor* and help other young people decide which careers were the best match for them! That young man's name was Heinz Ansbacher, and that is exactly what he did. Later, he returned to school for additional training to become a psychologist. Later still, he and his wife, Rowena, would become editors of *The Individual Psychology of Alfred Adler*, the foremost edition of the key writings of Alfred Adler, who was the namesake of my own doctoral school in psychology, and, if you haven't guessed, the man who told young Ansbacher what he should do with his life!

Let's analyze this story through the lenses of humility and magnanimity. Now young Heinz surely displayed humility in seeking out Adler's advice, but did Adler display humility when giving him the answer? At first glance, it might certainly appear not. Adler had never met the man before and in just a few minutes he presumed he could tell him what to do with his life.

Well, Adler was incredibly astute in his analysis of people's psychological issues. Indeed, sometimes he would hold open clinics in which people would present to him their problems, and he was usually able to provide them with very helpful insights, but he always did so in the most humble way. In fact, he was famous for ending each of his insightful analyses with a German phrase which translates into English like this: "Of course, everything could also be different!" In other words, he acknowledged that he might well be flat-out wrong, but he had given the situation his best effort. (I must admit that when I completed the last essay question of my written qualifying examination for Adler University, I ended it with Adler's famous phrase in the German[60]—and they still passed me.) Adler himself compelled no one to acknowledge his genius or follow his advice.

Further, even his method of questioning patients spoke of humility. He would not say, for example, "Your sense of inferiority in comparison to your sister's academic abilities is prompting you to act out to get attention," but he would always start his questions with a phrase like "Could it be?" He was not claiming to completely understand a person's situation but asking if the person had considered the possible reasons he gave.

Now as for magnanimity, the humility embodied by Ansbacher and Adler did not prevent them in the least from stretching their minds toward great things! The truly magnanimous person strives for great and honorable things, not so he will be honored by others but because the things he seeks are worthy and noble in themselves. Further, *he also wishes the same for his neighbor.* Such a person will strive to help his neighbor achieve worthy things as well, through benevolent assistance. Many in the world have benefited greatly from the humility and magnanimity of Alfred Adler and Heinz Ansbacher (and I'm happy to be one of them!).

How Humility Magnifies Magnanimity

Moving back from Adler to Aquinas—in comparing, contrasting, and reconciling humility and magnanimity, Thomas penetrates deep into the heart of both of them for us. Let's take in a few highlights.

St. Thomas examines humility over the course of six articles in the second part of the second part of his great *Summa Theologica*, question 161, appropriately titled "Humility." In the course of his first article, "Whether Humility Is a Virtue," Thomas presents a series of five "objections" (flawed arguments some people had put forth over time to say humility was *not* a virtue), and the third one reads like this: "Further, no virtue is opposed to another virtue. But humility is apparently opposed to the virtue of magnanimity, which aims at great things, whereas humility shuns them. Therefore it would seem that humility is not a virtue."

Thomas begins his answer to this and the other objections by talking about "difficult goods." When our appetites are drawn toward some truly worthy thing, achieving it is not always easy. As the philosopher Spinoza later put it so well, "All things excellent are as difficult as they are rare." So, when we try to obtain some difficult good, our appetites are *attracted* by its *goodness*, but *repelled* by the *difficulty* in obtaining it.

A simple example might be our feelings as we start on the attainment of an advanced academic degree. How nice it would be to have new knowledge and skills, not to mention those letters after our name, but oh, how daunting to think about just how much difficult work lies ahead of us!

How about another example (inspired by my hardworking wife)? Perhaps, like St. Thérèse, you're a lover of flowers. How grand it would be if at least one little section in your backyard blossomed with scents and colors, like your own little Garden of Eden to enjoy with your family and friends! After all, God so graciously gave us "every plant yielding seed which is upon the face of all the earth" (Genesis 1:29). Ah, but look at all those rocks and weeds and that stump that needs digging out. How *attractive* your potential garden's beauty, but how *repelling*, perhaps, is all that hard work!

So where do we go from here? Thomas says for desires that move us toward some good thing or goal we need a moral virtue that can *restrain* or moderate that impulse to make sure it is within our capacities and in keeping with right reason. For good things that repel us or make us recoil because of their difficulty, we need a moral virtue that will *strengthen* our appetite "and urge it on." Let's allow him to lay this all out:

> Wherefore a twofold virtue is necessary with regard to the difficult good; one, to temper and restrain the mind, lest it tend to high things immoderately; and this belongs to the virtue of humility: and another to strengthen the mind against despair, and urge it on to the pursuit of great things according to right reason; and this is magnanimity. Therefore it is evident that humility is a virtue.[61]

St. Thomas masterfully dispels any conflict between magnanimity and humility by calling to our attention both the divinely given and the fallen elements of our humanity. We have been given great and unique powers from God, and yet our fallen human nature is so readily prone to sin.

Magnanimity reflects our consideration of that divine spark within us, the recognition that we are greatly blessed by God and should use our powers for the greatest works within our capacities. We should not hide our lamps "under a bushel" but let our light "shine before men" (Matthew 5:15–16; see Mark 4:21–22; Luke 8:16–18). As we saw, we should not bury our talents but multiply them (Matthew 25:14–30; Luke 19:11–27). Magnanimity inspires us to undertake honorable yet difficult tasks. Indeed, we saw that it is not the virtue of humility but the *vice* of pusillanimity (smallness of soul) that leaves our lamps hidden and our talents underground.

Humility reflects the recognition of the weakness of our human nature. It recognizes that while we must always strive to do great things and make ourselves "perfect" as Christ instructed (Matthew 5:48), we never fully achieve that state in this life. Further, even the progress we do make is not entirely of our own doing but is enabled by God's grace. Humility reminds us not to be overly confident in our own, unaided powers. As Ben Sira has advised us, "Seek not what is too difficult for you (Sirach 3:21), and in this verse, so dear to this aging weight lifter's heart: "Do not lift a weight beyond your strength" (Sirach 13:2).

Humility speaks through Abraham: "Behold, I have taken upon myself to speak to the Lord, I whom am but dust and ashes" (Genesis 18:27), as magnanimity does through St. Paul: "I can do all things in him who strengthens me" (Philippians 4:13). Their words do not contradict each other but speak to what we truly are: lowly in nature, yet lifted high through God's grace. Thomas pithily resolves the apparent contradiction between humility and magnanimity as follows:

> It is contrary to humility to aim at greater things through confiding in one's own powers: but to aim at greater things through confidence in God's help, is not contrary to humility; especially since the more one subjects oneself to God, the more is one exalted in God's sight.[62]

So what should we make of humility and magnanimity in our modern times when popular culture advises us to achieve success and fame, to "look out for number one" and to "win at all costs" because "winning isn't everything ... it's the only thing"? Well, as far as competitiveness goes, these virtues goad us on not toward defeating others but toward defeating our own sinful nature, not necessarily toward climbing a secular ladder of success but toward climbing a ladder of spiritual perfection. Further, when we exercise the virtues of humility and magnanimity, we also recognize that *God has provided the potential for greatness of soul in every one of our neighbors*, as much as, or more than, he has for ourselves.

Humility Builds Patience

There is more to fortitude than magnanimity alone, though. It is also aided by the virtue of *magnificence*, whereby we strive to make great things through a willingness to expend our financial and other resources. (The Latin word for "to make" is *facere*, from which we derive "manufacture.") Still, per Thomas, "the principal act of fortitude is endurance, that is to stand immovable in the midst of dangers rather than to attack them."[63] We will all encounter all kinds of difficulties throughout our lives that we cannot conquer but must cope with and endure, refusing to give up, even when the going gets tough. For some this might take the form of a chronic illness, the illness or loss of a loved one, financial difficulties, moral failures, or some kind of rejection or persecution from others.

Two virtues essential to the enduring aspect of fortitude are *patience* and *perseverance.* We display the virtue of patience when we put up with difficulties, especially perhaps difficulties brought about by the annoying behaviors of others, without lashing out at them or experiencing sorrow or defeat ourselves. We display the virtue of perseverance when we persist in a difficult task over a great length of time, even if the going gets rougher and tougher.

And how does *humility* undergird patience?

The Saint Whose Humility Built Patience—and Loved Patients

In one of her ecstatic visions, God told St. Catherine of Siena that "a man proves his patience on his neighbor, when he receives injuries from him."[64] To say that a person "has the patience of a saint" likely implies that he or she has borne, with gentle grace, disrespect or ingratitude from another, perhaps a person he or she was striving mightily to help. Recalling that the great author on humility Fr. Cajetan Mary da Bergamo wrote that humility is common to every saint, we can recognize that it is the virtue of humility that enables saints to think so little of defending themselves that they can bear with patience and with love any slings and arrows their neighbors throw their way.

Let's look at how one particular saint took humility and patience to heavenly heights.

In the fourteenth century lived a most humble saint, one of twenty-five, yes *twenty-five*, children of a cloth dyer and his wife in the Tuscany region of Italy. Though she would receive virtually no formal education and never learned to write, she would become one of the Church's most beloved and important saints, a saint who influenced popes and even helped bring about the return of the Holy See to Rome after decades in Avignon, France.

Now, the saint of our story loved to love her neighbor by caring for the sick and dying. In one famous incident, our saint heard of a woman in the hospital with very advanced cancer. Due to the limited medical treatment of that time, the woman had an open wound that emitted such a stench that few people would come near her to care for her or even talk to her.

Blessed Raymond of Capua, our saint's confessor and biographer, wrote that once our saint heard of the woman's plight "she realized that heaven had reserved this unfortunate woman especially for herself"[65] and immediately sought her out. At times our saint would fight back physical nausea, but she persisted in caring for this patient day after day after day. After a while, the patient herself became abusive of our saint and began to spread lies dishonoring her purity. Our saint continued to care for the woman and instantly forgave her when she asked for forgiveness.

Indeed, our saint knew well, as St. Catherine of Siena would write, that a person builds patience by humbly enduring insults from our neighbors. She knew well because she *was* St. Catherine of Siena.

How Humility Tempers Temperance: From Cream-Filled Donuts to Fresh, Crisp Apples

Thomas notes that humility has a most particular relationship with one of the four cardinal virtues. That virtue is *temperance*, sometimes called self-control or moderation, that works to temper, control, or moderate, if you will, what is called the "concupiscible appetite," basically, our natural appetite and desires for various pleasures. These include some of the most basic and vehement physical appetites like those involved in eating, drinking, and sexual behaviors. These appetites are very good things in themselves, since we as individuals would die if we did not eat or drink, and we would die out as a species if we did not reproduce.

But as every human after the Fall has come to know, these appetites can be very powerful and difficult to control. For a simple example, for anyone who has cast aside a pledge to start eating right at the first sight of a cream-filled donut, the words of St. Paul will ring clear: "For I do not do what I want, but I do the very thing I hate" (Romans 7:15). Bringing powerful *appetites* under the control of *right reason* is the arduous task of temperance. Still, we should note well that temperance does not seek to destroy pleasure but to rein in our desires for pleasures that would destroy us. Further, temperance can serve to rein in not only our carnal or bodily desires but inappropriate *spiritual* strivings as well, and this is where humility really gets down to business.

We get a very clear picture of how a lack of humility can lead to failures in self-control in the first pages of Genesis. Note that the Serpent tempts Eve to eat the fruit from the forbidden Tree of the Knowledge of Good and Evil by telling her, "When you eat of it your eyes will be opened, and you will be like God, knowing good and evil" (Genesis 3:5). Christ would make clear centuries later to Adam and Eve's descendants that the devil is "a liar and the father of lies" (John 8:44), but Eve took the bait hook, line, and sinker, temped to become "like God." She ignored the fact that she and her spouse had already been crafted in God's own image (Genesis 1:27) and that through their endowments of intellect and will they already possessed the capacity to know good and evil as befits God's highest creature on earth. Eve hoped to be more than a creature and equal to the Creator himself (the thing that produced Satan's own fall). This is a supreme example of the kind of "immoderate" hope that Thomas told us needs the virtue of humility to temper it and rein it in!

As fallen descendants of Adam and Eve, we will find that the more we strive to grow in humility, the more our inappropriate desires to become or to achieve what is not fitting for us will diminish, and the more our appreciation for what God has already granted us and promises us one day will grow and grow. For even though we are fallen and must battle against our desires while here on earth, the Word of God Incarnate descended to earth for us, died for us, and ascended to heaven again so that, should we become gentle and lowly like him, we will someday ascend to heaven to join him.

How Humility Can Outshine Even Justice

The *Catechism* tells us that "justice consists in the firm and constant will to give God and neighbor their due" (CCC 1836). St. Thomas said justice, at its core, has two "integral" or essential parts that can be stated simply enough as "do good and do not do evil." He also described two "subjective parts" of justice, those being the primary subject matters to which justice is directed. The first, at least, will surely ring some bells.

Distributive justice is the relation between a whole to its parts. It refers to that way in which a community (a whole) distributes common goods to each individual (its parts). It bears a close relationship to what we hear about so much in our day under the label of "social justice." In the words of the *Catechism*, "Society ensures social justice when it provides the conditions that allow associations or individuals to obtain what is their due, according to their nature and their vocation. Social justice is linked to the common good and the exercise of authority" (CCC 1928).

Commutative justice is the second major form of justice. It regards the relation of one part to another. It refers to private individuals and the mutual dealings between them. Though we may not hear about it as much, it is extremely important, because acts of commutative justice are possible for each one of us every day as we relate to the individual human beings within our own lives. We are called to exercise this person-to-person justice regardless of how just or unjust we may believe the institutions within our society to be. Indeed, the *Catechism* makes its foundational importance quite clear: "Without commutative justice, no other form of justice is possible" (CCC 2411).

When Thomas elaborates on justice, he describes a panoply of "annexed" or "allied" virtues to bring it to its fullness in our daily lives, including the virtues of *religion* (what we owe to God), *piety* (what we owe to our parents and to our nation, our fatherland or motherland), *observance* (the *dulia* or honor and obedience we owe to those who excel us in some way or are in a position of higher authority), *gratitude* (the thanks we owe to all who help us), *truth* (which we owe to all), *friendliness* (the general affability and goodwill we owe to every person we meet), and *liberality* (the willingness to give freely from our surplus to people who are in need). We will pay a visit to many of justice's wonderful allies in the pages ahead, but for now we will return to justice itself and how it relates to humility.

Justice is the moral virtue that relates most directly not merely to how we control *our own passions*, but how we relate to *other people*. It is sometimes considered the exemplar of moral virtue. To say that a person is just is high moral praise indeed. The ancient Roman Cicero called justice "the most resplendent of the virtues."[66] Even the sometimes stolid Aristotle, the "father of logic" and all, waxed eloquent in praising this virtue: "The most excellent of the virtues would seem to be justice, and more glorious than either the evening or the morning star."[67] And yet, if you were attentive to our section heading, you will recall that I propose humility outshines even justice. Let's turn to the Angelic Doctor and to the "golden-mouthed" Church Father and Doctor to see just how brightly humility shines.

How Humility and Sin Crossed the Finish Line Before Justice and Pride

The great fourth-century Eastern Church Doctor St. John Chrysostom was so eloquent in his preaching that he was honored with the name Chrysostom—"Golden-Mouthed," from the Greek words *chrysos* for gold and *stoma* for mouth! When explaining the nature of humility, as well as singing the praises of its greatness, St. Thomas provided an interesting little thought experiment found in Chrysostom's sermons. Allow me to put it in their words:

> Hence Chrysostom says: "Bring me a pair of two-horse chariots: in the one harness pride with justice, in the other sin with humility: and you will see that sin outrunning justice wins not by its own strength, but by that of humility: while you will see the other pair beaten, not by the weakness of justice, but by the weight and size of pride."[68]

Thomas says the moral of this interesting little hypothetical horse race is not to put down justice or to set humility above it but to show that if justice is coupled with the sin of pride, justice is no longer a virtue. For example, if we were to treat someone fairly not because we care about his or her rightful due but so that others would think we are just, we would have exercised not justice but pride within our souls.

Further, "sin is pardoned through humility: for it is said of the publican (Luke 18:14) that through the merit of humility 'he went down into his house justified.'"[69] Therefore, we see that in Chrysostom's horse race, justice has been stripped of its virtue by teaming up with the ponderous evil ally of pride, while the burden of sin has been lifted and purified through the healing merits of humility.

Every one of us is called to treat justly every person we meet, but we should not pride ourselves on how just we are or boldly signal our virtue to others. Rather, our justice should rest on the firm foundation of humility. We should give each person his or her rightful due not for the honor it might bring our way but because we recognize that every other person deserves to be treated justly, just as much as we desire just treatment ourselves.

Docility, Through Humility, Unleashes Ability

St. Thomas has described a virtue that works in the service of intellectual humility specifically to perfect our powers of learning from others—the virtue of *docility*. In our time, docility, like humility, may suggest a passivity or submissiveness, but note that the word derives from the Latin *docere*, "to teach," and means a willingness to be taught. With an attitude directly opposed to a listless passivity, the truly docile person does not merely sit there awaiting instructions but actively thirsts for true knowledge and for people who can teach it. It takes humility to admit we have so much to learn and to admit that others may know some important things much more extensively and deeply than we do—that they have advanced along the path of science (knowledge), far beyond where we have. Indeed, Thomas wrote that "a characteristic of one possessing science is the ability to teach."[70]

Docile for Life

Indeed, even after we are finished with school, we *all* remain students in dire need of docility when it comes to the things that truly matter the most, things like "the three H's," we might say, of humility, holiness, and heaven.

In regards to those things that matter the most, the Scriptures advise us again and again to be open to learning from *other people* who are more learned than we. Here are a few examples:

- "Hear, O sons, a father's instruction, and be attentive, that you may gain insight; for I give you good precepts: do not forsake my teaching" (Proverbs 4:1–2).

- "Without counsel plans go wrong, but with many advisers they succeed" (Proverbs 15:22).

- "The mind of the wise man will ponder the words of the wise" (Sirach 3:29).

- "Be ready to listen to every narrative, and do not let wise proverbs escape you. If you see an intelligent man, visit him early; let your foot wear out his doorstep" (Sirach 6:35–36).

And we must always remain docile to the Ultimate Source of all wisdom, understanding, and knowledge:

- "The LORD by wisdom founded the earth; by understanding he established the heavens; by his knowledge the deeps broke forth, and the clouds drop down the dew" (Proverbs 3:19–20).

- "Talk no more so very proudly, let not arrogance come from your mouth; for the LORD is a God of knowledge" (1 Samuel 2:3).

- "Reflect on the statutes of the Lord, and meditate at all times on his commandments. It is he who will give insight to your mind, and your desire for wisdom will be granted" (Sirach 6:37).

- "Learn from me; for I am gentle and lowly in heart, and you will find rest for your souls. For my yoke is easy, and my burden is light" (Matthew 11:29–30).

The Charioteer of the Virtues

St. Thomas describes the cardinal virtue of *prudence*, or practical wisdom, as "right reason in action." The *Catechism* calls prudence the *auriga virtutum*, or "charioteer of the virtues" (CCC 1806). It's an interesting coincidence that we find ourselves back to chariots again, but this time our virtue is not one of the steeds but the driver!

Thomas says that prudence is *both* an intellectual virtue aimed at *truth* and a moral virtue aimed at achieving *good*. While *sapientia* (wisdom) is the highest intellectual virtue aimed at the highest truths in themselves, *prudentia*'s special role is to *apply* wisdom to the actions of our daily lives. It is about finding virtuous means to the virtuous ends we seek. It guides the other moral virtues, for example by helping us learn how to express courage, or *fortitude*, in the right situations, when we should *temper* or restrain our desires and when we shouldn't, and just what kinds of acts are truly *just* in particular situations.

Thomas elaborates that prudence is forward-looking because it aims at future goals, but it does this by recalling important moral lessons from the past, and by understanding how they apply in current situations. Both

Cicero and St. Albert, Thomas' great teacher, elaborated on three "parts" of prudence being *providentia* (foresight) that looks forward, *memoria* (memory) that retains lessons from past experience, and *intellectus* (intellect or understanding) that applies abstract moral principles to concrete, real-life situations in the present. In short, to achieve virtuous goals in the future, we must act rightly in the present, guided by moral lessons from the past.

Borrowing from other philosophers and theologians, St. Thomas listed a full eight "integral" (essential) parts. To *foresight, memory,* and *understanding*, he also added *shrewdness* (the ability to think quickly on one's feet when necessary), *reason* (the ability to apply knowledge to new things), *circumspection* (the ability to look all around at factors relevant to a decision), and *caution* (the ability to avoid obstacles to one's goals). The eighth virtue necessary for prudence is precisely the kind of intellectual humility we have been talking about—*docility* itself.

Thomas says we must always strive for perfect docility and even the mature man "must carefully, frequently and reverently apply his mind to the teachings of the learned, neither neglecting them through laziness, nor despising them through pride." Further, "even the learned should be docile in some respects, since no man is altogether self-sufficient in matters of prudence."[71]

OK, so it is through docility that humility plays an essential role within prudence. Are there more parts to prudence? Well, Thomas, being ever so thorough, also described three other virtues that are "connected with prudence, and which are its quasi-potential parts."[72]

Quasi-potential parts? Well, they are virtues that aid prudence sometimes under specific situations. Since they were identified by Aristotle, Thomas addresses them in the Greek. *Synesis* refers to the ability to make right judgments about practical matters. Thomas said people with *synesis* are said to show "good sense." *Gnome* refers not to little bearded men in one's garden, but to the ability to exercise right judgment in extreme or unusual cases. (Perhaps King Solomon's effective decision to cut in two the baby of the disputing mothers is a prime biblical example of *gnome* in action. See 1 Kings 3:16–28 for the whole story.)

Humility Seeks Good Counsel

Last but not least is our "quasi-potential virtue" with direct ties to prudence and also to humility—namely, *eubolia,* which comes from the Greek words meaning "good counsel." Thomas says prudence operates in a three-step process.

Our first step in exercising prudence is to *consider alternative courses of action*, which we do through *eubolia*, by consulting with wiser advisers who can help us make the best choices. The proud and imprudent are known for skipping this virtue. Remember: "The way of a fool is right in his own eyes, but a wise man listens to advice" (Proverbs 12:15).

Now, once we have exercised *eubolia* by seeking counsel and considering our alternative courses of action, we judge the best alternative, courtesy of *synesis*. Finally, we issue the self-command to act on that judgment, which is indeed the defining act of prudence itself.

Let's consider an example of taking the best care of our bodily temples. So your doctor has told you that some things in your last blood test are out of whack and could cause health problems sometime down the line. What would be the prudent thing to do?

Well, first you might exercise *humility*, by acknowledging that you are not the doctor and you need good expert advice (*eubolia*) about what you should do. The first likely stop is that doctor him- or herself. Perhaps his or her first suggestion is a medication. You might ask more questions, seeking advice about possible side effects or if particular lifestyle changes in your diet or exercise might be worth trying first. If you feel unsure about the answers you receive, obtaining a second opinion from another expert might be a prudent thing to do. At some point, you will have to judge which option seems best for you (*synesis*) and then command yourself (the final act of prudence) to follow what appear to be the best orders.

So in both physical and spiritual matters, if we desire to determine and carry out the most prudent acts in our daily lives, the humility that undergirds *docility* and *eubolia* will provide our virtuous "charioteer" with the very best directions to "finish the race," as St. Paul might say (see 2 Timothy 4:7), the race to eternal life.

How Humility Unwraps the *Gifts* of Fortitude, Fear, Piety, and Counsel

We have taken a look at how humility helps the four cardinal virtues fly high, and now we will take a quick peek at how humility helps unwrap four gifts of the Holy Spirit that perfect each of the four cardinal virtues.

Would you believe that theologians have determined the gift of the Holy Spirit that perfects the *virtue* of fortitude is the *gift* of, well, fortitude? (I thought you would.)

Recalling that fortitude derives from the word meaning strength, can we think of anything that could possibly be stronger than strength that comes from God himself? Through the virtue of fortitude we use the powers of our own reason and the strength of our own bodies to overcome or at least endure difficult obstacles. Of course, we may not always emerge victorious. The brave soldier imbued with fortitude may well still fall before his enemy.

The Gift That Never Fails

Yet, the Holy Spirit's gift of fortitude, if embraced, never fails to overcome the most difficult obstacles of all to obtain the highest of all goods, eternal bliss in heaven. This is seen most clearly in the case of martyrs who die for the Faith. This willingness to suffer even death for the Faith is made possible by the gift of fortitude, a gift that carries them to the highest realms of heaven. In this sense, the Holy Spirit's gift of fortitude defeats even death itself.

St. Thomas says that through the gift of fortitude our hope is buoyed because a "certain confidence" is "infused into the mind" regarding our ultimate victory in life since we willingly submit to the Holy Spirit's guidance.[73]

Thankfully, you and I are probably not called to be martyrs, but as St. Thomas notes, "he that stands firm against great things, will in consequence stand firm against less things."[74] The Holy Spirit's gift of fortitude can help us endure and persevere through all kinds of trials in our daily lives.

What role does humility play here? To fully embrace the Holy Spirit's gift of fortitude, we must admit the limitations of our own strength and ask God to assist us with his mighty arm in our struggles. When we recognize how weak we are on our own, we open our souls to God's immeasurable strength.

How a Lack of Humility Both Bound and "Unlocked" Samson's Power[75]

Samson, the famous strong man of biblical times, received his might as the Holy Spirit's gift. We hear that "the Spirit of the LORD came mightily upon him" (Judges 14:19; 15:14) as he went on to fight and defeat up to a thousand enemies.

If you know the story, you may recall that Samson, who achieved great fame and notoriety due to his mighty feats, decided to pursue a beautiful woman named Delilah. Delilah began asking Samson why he was so strong. The true reason for his strength was that he was dedicated to the Lord, and, as part of that dedication, no one had ever cut his hair. But Samson did not tell Delilah this—at first. When he told her, falsely, that he could be overcome if he was bound with seven bowstrings, Delilah tried it, planning to hand him over to his enemies, the Philistines. Yet instead of leaving the treacherous woman, Samson remained with her, and a similar scene played out a second time and even a third time. But the fourth time, Samson gave in and revealed his secret to Delilah. Then he could not escape because Delilah saw to it that his hair was gone, and so he was captured by the Philistines.

Considering this sequence of events, as I have written elsewhere, the great thirteenth-century Franciscan Church Doctor St. Bonaventure explained that "there are four pleasures of the senses" by which the gifts of the Holy Spirit are lost: "attention, thought, the inclination of the inner affections, and the rejection of the divine laws."[76]

When Samson was bound the first time at Delilah's hands, it represented how the Devil tempted him through "the delights of the senses." The second repetition of the scene mirrored the way Samson failed to reject temptation but toyed with the sensual pleasures in his mind. In the third attempt by Delilah to overcome him, she wove his hair tightly to a loom. This represented the way he was held fast to low things by his thoughts.

Instead of obeying the Lord out of love, Samson chiefly loved Delilah, who betrayed him. In consequence, he lost his strength that the Lord had given him. St. Bonaventure draws a comparison between the *seven* gifts of the Holy Spirit and the *seven* locks of Samson's hair that meant he was filled with the Lord's power (see Judges 16:19)—and, likewise, Delilah used *seven* ropes in her effort to overcome Samson.

But the story did not end there. When Samson's hair grew again, he prayed for God's help to perform a last feat of strength. No longer distracted by earthly pleasures, he once again humbled himself before the Lord. With God's help, he destroyed the place where the Philistines were celebrating, though he knew it would cost him his life in the process.

This intriguing lesson about the gifts of the Holy Spirit shows us what happens when even a great man loses humility, and it also shows us that it is never too late in this life to ask God for his graces again.

Humility and Fear of the Lord

The virtue of humility as allied with the virtue of *temperance* has traditionally been linked most closely to the Holy Spirit's gift of *fear of the Lord*. Just ask St. Thomas, who addresses humility as a virtue allied with temperance (and ask St. Augustine, too):

> Wherefore humility would seem to denote in the first place man's subjection to God; and for this reason Augustine (De Serm. Dom. in Monte i, 4 [*Our Lord's Sermon On the Mount* 1.4]) ascribes humility, which he understands by poverty of spirit, to the gift of fear whereby man reveres God.[77]

The stronger our fear and reverence of God, the greater will our capacity be to rein in our passions and to battle against sins of desire. Note too how St. Augustine paired humility with Christ's great beatitude of *poverty of spirit*. And what is God's gift for those with true poverty of spirit? Christ told us, "Theirs is the kingdom of heaven" (Matthew 5:3).

Indeed, Thomas provides some intriguing insights on the relationship between poverty of spirit and humility when he considers who will assist Christ at the Final Judgment. Building upon Job 36:6, "He saveth not the wicked, and He giveth judgment to the poor,"[78] Thomas notes among other observations that those who embrace voluntary poverty warrant exceptional merit because of their humility. Further: "Now of all the things that make man contemptible in this world humility is the chief: and for this reason the excellence of judicial power is promised to the poor, so that he who humbles himself for Christ's sake shall be exalted."[79]

May the Lord humble our hearts and open them up to the Holy Spirit's great gift of fear of the Lord.

How Humble Pie(ty) Perfects Justice

And what gift corresponds most closely to *justice*? St. Thomas proposes the gift of *piety*. You might recall he described the virtue of piety as a virtue that supports the virtue of justice by giving our parents and our nation the respect and service they are rightfully due. Well, through the Holy Spirit's gift of piety we not only fear the Lord as *our Almighty Creator*, we revere and love him as *our loving Father*.

So, ironically, when we humble ourselves to remember our lowly origin and total dependence upon God for our existence, it opens us to the realization that he has called *us* to be his *spiritually adopted children*. Note, too, that when God's only begotten Son taught us how to pray, his very first words were "Our Father" (Matthew 6:9). May we humble ourselves before God our Father so that his Holy Spirit may shower us with the gift of piety!

Counsel Is Prudence of the Holy Spirit

And finally, as to *prudence*, a most perfect of perfecting gifts is found in the Holy Spirit's gift of *counsel*. Indeed, John of St. Thomas has called this gift "the prudence of the Spirit."[80] You'll recall that in exercising *eubolia* we seek the wise counsel of other human beings. Well, through the Holy Spirit's gift of counsel, we seek and obtain the unerring counsel of the Holy Spirit himself. His counsel might directly provide us the prudent answers to complex real-life situations we face, or he may choose to guide us to the right human advisers. Either way, we are unlikely to hear God's "still small voice" (1 Kings 19:12) of counsel if we are too busy and prideful trying to figure out everything on our own.

Humility's Holy Toolbox:

The Cardinal Virtues of Living

1. **Pray** for the cardinal virtues. Here are some words that St. Thomas used:

    > Lord, "grant that I may through justice be subject to You, through prudence avoid the beguilements of the devil, through temperance exercise restraint, and through fortitude endure adversity with patience. Grant that whatever good things I have, I may share generously with those who have not and that whatever good things I do not have, I may request humbly from those who do."[81]

    And pray for the Holy Spirit's gifts of fear of the Lord, piety, fortitude, and counsel that can help those four cardinals fly all the way to heaven. The great eighteenth-century Church Doctor St. Alphonsus Liguori prayed for these four gifts like this:

    > "O Giver of all supernatural gifts, who filled the soul of the Blessed Virgin Mary, Mother of God, with such immense favors, I beg You to visit me with Your grace and Your love and to grant me the gift of holy fear, so that it may act on me as a check to prevent me from falling back into my past sins, for which I beg pardon. Grant me the gift of piety, so that I may serve You for the future with increased fervor, follow with more promptness Your holy inspirations, and observe your divine precepts with greater fidelity ... Grant me the gift of fortitude, so that I may overcome courageously all the assaults

of the devil, and all the dangers of this world which threaten the salvation of my soul. Grant me the gift of counsel, so that I may choose what is more conducive to my spiritual advancement and may discover the wiles and snares of the tempter."[82]

2. **Embrace** the sacrament of Confirmation. St. Thomas said that "Confirmation is to Baptism as growth to birth."[83] Humility would not keep us as spiritual babies but spurs us on to grow into mature warriors of the Faith. We are confirmed by a bishop, and that is significant. Per Thomas: "Though he who is baptized is made a member of the Church, nevertheless he is not yet enrolled as a Christian soldier. And therefore he is brought to the bishop, as to the commander of the army."[84] Confirmation means "make firm" or strengthen and therefore has a special relationship with the virtue and gift of fortitude.

Indeed, in this sacrament, the bishop prays, "Send your Holy Spirit upon them to be their helper and guide. Give them the spirit of wisdom and understanding, the spirit of right judgment and courage, the spirit of knowledge and reverence. Fill them with the spirit of wonder and awe in your presence," and during the anointing he prays, "Be sealed with the gift of the Holy Spirit."

So let us take time now and then to humbly reflect on the great gifts of our Confirmation. Though God fashioned us from the clay of the earth, he not only breathed life into our souls, but through the graces of his Church, he breathes his own Holy Spirit into us as well. We should be literally "inspired" to embrace all the virtues and gifts of living to do all the good that we can for the greater glory of God.

Chapter 2 Summary and Reflections

Humility not only helps perfect our intellects by opening our minds to *truth*, it perfects our hearts and our wills as well, undergirding the moral virtues through which we do *good* in accordance with God's will. Humility can help us rein in illicit desires by undergirding temperance, overcome fears and summon up the courage to do hard things through strengthening fortitude, keep us focused on noble goals through the virtue of magnanimity built on our confidence in Christ, treat each other as patiently and as justly as we would have them treat us, and through a willingness to learn and to take advice from others to live good lives bearing fruits of meekness and practical wisdom. Humility is also the verdant soil from which the Holy Spirit's gifts of fear of the Lord, fortitude, piety, and counsel can grow and thrive within our souls.

Let's ask questions like the following:

- Is there some good but difficult task I am fearful of doing because I am afraid of what others might think if I fail? If so, can I pray to God to give me the humility to set my fragile ego aside and focus instead on doing whatever hard work it takes to complete the task he has set before me?

- Am I struggling reining in some kind of illicit bodily or spiritual desire, be it sensual pleasure or a desire for fame or prestige? If so, am I willing to call in humility, fear of the Lord, and poverty of spirit to buttress my temperance and rein in my hope for inappropriate pleasures or goals?

- Have I used a false humility as an excuse for habits of pusillanimity? In other words, is there some area in which I have *used humility as an excuse* to keep me from giving my all to utilize the talents and gifts God has given me to make great things happen for his glory?

- Have I proudly signaled to others my virtue of justice on social media platforms or in conversations by decrying institutional or societal injustices, while ignoring unjust logs within my own eyes, treating unjustly the people within my own daily life? If so, how can I give those people their rightful due *today*?

- When faced with important decisions, do I boldly "do it my way," or am I docile enough to seek out the counsel of wise men and women?

- Can I set aside a brief time each day, maybe even before arising from bed, to ask the Holy Spirit to help me today to humbly listen to God's "still small voice" of counsel and guidance for the tasks I will face in the day ahead?

Humility Lived Saint Story #2:

St. Patrick of Ireland (c. 389–461)

I, Patrick, am a sinner, the most uncultured and smallest among all the faithful, indeed many people consider me to be worthless.[85]

–St. Patrick, *Confession*

Everyone knows St. Patrick, and many American cities celebrate the feast of his death on earth and birth in heaven every March 17. A highly influential man, this great saint reached the hearts of the people of Ireland so that they rejected their pagan religion and followed Christ, the One whom Patrick followed. Ancient lives of St. Patrick from the Middle Ages burst with pious legends of astonishing miracles, and yet the quote above shows how Patrick spoke of himself in his own brief *Confession*, which provides what is likely the most accurate information we have on his life.

Remarkable indeed that Patrick, powerful over the forces of evil and known for his miracles, calls himself "worthless" in the eyes of others! St. Patrick was truly a man in whom humility ran deep, and so, therefore, did the cardinal virtues and their associated gifts. Let's zoom in on a few of the moral virtues this great saint displayed to the most heroic degree.

Humility and Perseverance

Patrick was kidnapped from Britain by Irish pirates at around the age of sixteen. Although his father was a deacon, Patrick did not practice his faith deeply until his nearly seven years of captivity. There he learned the humility to reach out to the Lord, whom he said he prayed to one hundred times per day and as many times per night, while working as a shepherd. He eventually escaped from Ireland and journeyed back to his home in Britain. After "a few short years," he tells us, he heard in a vision "the voice of the Irish" calling him to return to them.[86] From that point on he burned with desire to return to the land of his enslavement and to bring the Irish people to Christ.

Yet he never ranked himself among the learned, since he had spent his youth in slavery. For many years, he applied himself to gaining knowledge so that he would be ready to return to Ireland as a missionary and a bishop. In fact, he was in his forties or fifties when he finally arrived on the island bringing the truth of Christ. That's perseverance!

Prudence and Gratitude

Patrick needed more than even his burning desire and long-standing perseverance to win the Irish people to Christ. He needed the practical know-how to get the job done, and this is the realm of prudence. To build Christ's holy Church in Ireland, Patrick had to erect dozens upon dozens of church buildings as well. His humility told him he could not complete this vision alone, so he sought out the advice of others and assembled a team to take with him to accomplish both the spiritual and the physical tasks before them.

And once he arrived, his team grew by leaps and bounds through the Irish men and women he persuaded to join them through his humility, prudence, and love for Jesus Christ. Indeed, he often started his missions by converting local Irish chieftains and higher order kings, who would bring their people into the Church with them.

Here is one of my favorite little stories of how he got that job done. A king of an Irish province dispatched a messenger with a dish made of rich copper as a gift for Patrick, whose reputation had reached the king's ears. All Patrick said upon receiving this kingly gift was *"Deo gratias"* ("Thanks be to God").[87] Taking offense because Patrick had not mentioned him as giver, the king reclaimed the dish. All Patrick said as the rich gift was taken away was "Thanks be to God." The king was so moved by Patrick's willingness to thank God no matter the circumstances that he gave Patrick the copper dish once more and prepared to come in person to speak with the saint.

May God great us all some measure of the humility, perseverance, prudence, and gratitude of the patron saint of Ireland![88]

Chapter 3

HUMILITY LOVES GOD

*The theological virtues are the foundation of Christian moral
activity; they animate it and give it its special character ... They
are infused by God into the souls of the faithful to make them
capable of acting as his children and of meriting eternal life ...
There are three theological virtues: faith, hope, and charity.*

—Catechism of the Catholic Church 1813

The baptized person should train himself to live in humility.

—Catechism of the Catholic Church 2540

We saw in chapter 1 that St. Thomas said, "Humility, considered as a
special virtue, regards chiefly the subjection of man to God."[89] Well,
regarding the three most special virtues of all, the *theological virtues,* our
Catechism tells us, "They have the One and Triune God for their origin,
motive, and object" (CCC 1812).

How the Least and the Highest of Virtues Look Toward God

These virtues—faith, hope, and charity—are the most special virtues of all because they transcend and perfect all human virtues. Deriving not from our human nature, "they are infused by God into the souls of the faithful to make them capable of acting as his children and of meriting eternal life" (CCC 1813). Further, they "adapt man's faculties for participation in the divine nature: for the theological virtues relate directly to God" (CCC 1812).

Perhaps such supernatural transcendence of human virtue will ring a bell if you recall our previous discussion of the gifts of the Holy Spirit. If so, very good, for St. Thomas tells us supernatural graces, including the Holy Spirit's gifts, "flow from" from the theological virtues God infuses into our souls.

Now, when does God first infuse faith, hope, and charity into our souls? Yes, indeed, at the time of our Baptism. The *Catechism* (1265–1266) tells us that Baptism makes us new creatures, adopted children of God with the sanctifying grace of *justification* that gives us faith in him, hope in him, and love for him through the theological virtues. It even goes on to specify that Baptism gives us the grace to "act under the prompting of the Holy Spirit through the gifts of the Holy Spirit" and "to grow in goodness through the moral virtues."

Note well too that while the theological virtues transcend and perfect all virtues, coming from God himself, we saw in our opening quotation that "the baptized person should train himself to live in humility" (CCC 2540). Humility remains a foundational virtue in every child of God. And though we are blessed with powerful graces from God, we still have our own job to do! We still have to cooperate with God's graces and *train ourselves* to live lives of humility. So again, we see that the lowliest of the virtues plays a very lofty role in the life of every baptized Christian, by actualizing the holy potentials God gives us through faith, hope, and charity. Let's look at them one by one and see how humility can help us *believe* in, *trust* in, and *love* God with all that we are.

Humility Believes

St. Paul tells us that "faith is the assurance of things hoped for, the conviction of things not seen" (Hebrews 11:1). The *Catechism* elaborates as follows: "Faith is the theological virtue by which we believe in God and believe all that he has said and revealed to us, and that Holy Church proposes for our belief, because he is truth itself" (CCC 1814). In contrasting the supernatural virtue of faith with the natural virtue of *religion* (a virtue allied to justice whereby we try to give God his rightful due to the extent that we can by worshipping him through internal and external actions), St. Thomas writes:

> And yet the acts whereby God is worshiped do not reach out to God himself, as when we believe God we reach out to Him by believing; for which reason it was stated (1, 1 and 2 and 4) that God is the object of faith, not only because we *believe in a God*, but because we *believe God*.[90]

The theological virtue of faith then does not oppose the natural moral virtue of religion but transforms it into a supernatural, intimate, personal relationship with God whom we believe because we know he is Truth itself.

Religion and faith are both clearly members of God's team, but unfortunately, perhaps more than ever before in our time, with the significant rise in unbelievers and "nones" (people with no religious affiliations at all), it is becoming a common and fatal misconception that the team of *science* and *reason* are enemies of *faith* and *religion.* Hopefully our treatment of the intellectual virtues, *science* among them, will help give the lie to such a false dichotomy, but we need to dig in deeper and to see the role humility can play in grasping the relationship of faith to reason. But first, a powerful true story. No, make that two!

Why the Modern "Pagan Eagle" and the "World's Most Notorious Atheist" Finally Flew to God

The "pagan eagle" refers to the second Dr. Adler we will meet in this book. The first was Alfred Adler, the psychiatrist for whom my doctoral school in psychology was named. The second is Mortimer Adler, the great twentieth-century philosopher and great books proponent.

And why is he described as the "pagan eagle"? Well, when Mortimer Adler wrote the book *How to Think About God* in 1980, he called himself a pagan. Further, "adler" is the German word for eagle. Finally, because it allowed for a quirky section heading that fit in Antony Flew's name as well.

As for our "pagan," Mortimer Adler, though a nonpracticing Jew for most of his life, always considered himself a Thomist in philosophy, a man with great respect for the philosophical approach of our own St. Thomas Aquinas. Adler proceeded to think so much about God that two years before his death, at the age of ninety-six, this Jewish-pagan-Thomist came home to the Church of St. Thomas, St. Peter, and Christ. In December of 1999, Dr. Adler, the *ex*-pagan, became a Catholic!

Adler concluded *How to Think About God* with a section entitled "Adverse Views," in which he cited books and articles by philosophers who disagreed with his thesis that reason leads to God. One was a book entitled *God and Philosophy* by distinguished British philosopher of religion Antony Flew. That book, published in 1966, was one of his many scholarly tomes propounding that reason leads to atheism. Well, as fate (no, God) would have it, forty-one years later, Professor Flew would write a book happily entitled *There Is a God: How the World's Most Notorious Atheist Changed His Mind*. Through his continued philosophical ponderings and musings on modern science, one of the world's foremost philosophers and revered champion of atheist circles came to abandon the "adverse views" camp.

Flew reversed his long-held positions, upon which much of his reputation as a philosopher of religion had been built. Now that took some humility! Noting that he, like Socrates, always held that he must go wherever the arguments led him, he found himself led to God (as Socrates himself had been). Flew also acknowledged that the God of Aristotle—unchanging, immaterial, omnipotent, omniscient, one, indivisible, perfectly good, and necessarily existing ("the god of the philosophers")—is also quite consistent with God as described within the Judeo-Christian tradition ("the God of Abraham, Isaac, and Jacob").

Flew wrote that he had no revelation or "personal experience of God ... In short, my discovery of the divine has been a pilgrimage of reason and not of faith." Yet even so, in a section labeled "Open to Learning More," he would comment that "no other religion enjoys anything like the combination of a charismatic figure like Jesus and a first class intellectual like St. Paul. If you're wanting omnipotence to set up a religion, it seems to me that this [Christianity] is the one to beat!"[91]

A key lesson both philosophers learned through the intellectual humility that undergirds rigorous *step-by-step reasoning*, is that faith is *not* unreasonable. Of the two though, only Adler added the final leap of faith to, in St. Thomas' words, not only *believe in* God but to *believe God* by embracing the Catholic Faith.

So now let's fan out our wings and take a broader look at the relationship between faith and reason—and *humility*.

Humility Has Faith for Good Reasons

We have seen from Scripture and the *Catechism* that faith is about "things not seen" and about what God has revealed to us. In this sense faith transcends knowledge or science, which normally operate upon the evidence of our senses. Faith addresses immaterial, spiritual realities, like God and the angels, that cannot be directly seen by our eyes (unless the angels have assumed a physical body on some mission for God). Still, their existence is not opposed to the truths of reason and science, because there is but one truth. God allows no contradictions in reality.

Indeed, St. Thomas is famous for his five arguments for the existence of God that start with the *evidence of our senses*, such as the fact that things move or change, that there are causes and effects, that things exist for a time, that some things are more perfect than others, and that there is purposive action in the world. Next, using chains of what is called *a posteriori reasoning* (working backwards from effects to their causes), Thomas proves that there must be an Unmoved Mover, a First Efficient Cause, a Necessary Being, a Perfect Being, and a Final Cause or Purpose of all being, "and this we call God."[92] Indeed, this truth was confirmed at the First Vatican Council: "God, the first principle and last end of all things, can be known with certainty from the created world by the natural light of human reason."[93]

So faith and right reason are in clear agreement about the existence of God, although faith, based on God's divine revelation to man, penetrates God's reality far more deeply and intimately. As Fr. Garrigou-Lagrange once put it so aptly, "Faith may be likened to the sun, and science or knowledge to a candle, but nothing need prevent the sun and a candle from shedding light on the same object together."[94]

Revealed faith does not contradict science and reason, but it tells us things about God's majesty and glory that reason alone cannot fathom—for example, that God is a Trinity or that God the Son became incarnate on earth for our salvation. Therefore, even people who are convinced by reason of God's existence must take the proverbial leap of faith to believe that "the god of the philosophers," accessible to reason, is also "the God of Abraham, of Isaac, and of Jacob" (Exodus 3:6), as revealed in Scripture. It takes a leap of faith to believe that the Unmoved Mover, First Cause, and Necessary Being is the God who told Moses his name is "I AM WHO I AM" (Exodus 3:14), and to believe Jesus who said, "Before Abraham was, I am" (John 8:58).

Humility plays a crucial role in this fateful, faithful leap. The modern secular world, so bereft of humility and swollen with pride, increasingly says, "God, I don't need you!" or "You do not exist!" as it transgresses God's laws with man-made laws that no longer honor God or even the inherent dignity and right to life of every human. By substituting belief in human institutions and governments for belief in God, by imagining a world without religion, the secular world believes it can create its own heaven on earth. Yet its large-scale attempts at secular utopias, like the atheistic communist Soviet Union of the twentieth century, have buried millions under the earth and made life for those under their rule like hell on earth before their demise.

We all need humility in our personal, individual lives as Christians too, as so many who have presumed to live without God find their lives bereft of deep meaning and spiritual solace. But if we embrace humility and faith, we will not forget our origins from the lowly ground of the earth as we welcome the invitation to grow in union with God, the ground of all being.

May God grant us all the humility to make that leap of faith. May we *believe in* God, *believe* God, and grow in our knowledge of the teachings of the Faith so that we might live happy and holy lives on earth and one day in heaven see for ourselves those things we believe that are *for now* unseen.

Humility Hopes

St. Thomas describes the *natural power (or "passion") of hope* as our attraction toward the attainable but difficult good. Our natural capacity to hope is a very important thing indeed.

Sadly, I learned decades ago during my psychological training that one of the most powerful predictors of suicide is a strong and chronic sense of hopelessness, in which the profoundly depressed come to believe that the good they seek, a reasonably happy life, is forever too difficult and, indeed, impossible for them to attain.[95]

Happily, recent psychological studies have found that high levels of hope, the belief that one has what it takes to devise and carry out the plans to achieve one's goals, are associated with all kinds of positive outcomes in all kinds of areas, including academic and athletic performance, physical and mental health, responsiveness to psychotherapy, and helping inoculate children from feelings of loneliness.

Still, God has provided us with an infinitely more powerful form of hope, the kind of hope that trusts not on our own powers but on the powers of God to reach the arduous but loftiest goal of them all—an eternal life of bliss with him in heaven. This is the stuff of the God-infused *theological virtue of hope.*

The *Catechism* describes the two key elements of the virtue of hope as (1) desiring a life of eternal happiness with God, and (2) "placing our trust in Christ's promises and relying not on our own strength, but on the help of the grace of the Holy Spirit" (CCC 1817). In other words, the supernatural virtue of *hope entails our desire to spend eternity in heaven with God and our confidence that he will provide us all the help we need to get there.*

Do you see an immediate link here with humility? All the saints knew that they could not raise themselves to heaven by their own bootstraps but only through embracing the virtue of hope and a willing cooperation with the stirrings of the Holy Spirit within them.

One function of humility, then, is to rein in a perversion of hope known as the sin of *presumption,* which is classed as a sin against hope and a sin against the Holy Spirit. The *Catechism* tells us that we may presume either by overconfidence in our own ability to earn salvation without God's help or by presuming on God's omnipotence or mercy that he will grant us our salvation without any effort or merit on our part (CCC 2092). A person falsely buoyed by presumption is unlikely to strive to grow in virtue, to fight against sin, or to confess grave sins when committed. Sadly, he will find on Judgment Day that he had presumed wrongly. St. Thomas said that one of humility's jobs is to rein in *inappropriate hopes.* Presumption expresses the most inappropriate hope of all.

Clinging to Hope in the Treacherous Waters Between Scylla and Charybdis

The ancient Greeks told the myth of Scylla and Charybdis, two horrible perils at either side of a narrow passage in the Mediterranean Sea. Well, if presumption is the multi-headed monster to the one side of hope, *despair* is the swirling whirlpool on its other side. Through the sin of despair, we abandon our hope of salvation through our trust in God's goodness. Despair makes the sailors give up and toss hope over the side of the ship. Despair stills the oars of the virtues and furls the sails of the Holy Spirit's gifts, rejecting the winds that can guide us to heaven. Despair is the manifestation of a theological hopelessness that rejects the mercy of God and which may manifest a sordid sort of a prideful false humility (e.g., "*My* sins are so great, not even God almighty could forgive them!").

In his great *Summa Theologica,* when considering the eschatological question of whether souls in heaven and hell are ever permitted to leave it (short answer, yes, in specific instances where God permits it), Thomas cites a wonderful rhetorical question from St. Jerome who argued against those who thought such departures were impossible: "Wouldst thou then lay down the law for God?"[96] In a sense, if we presume upon God's mercy, ignoring his justice, or despair of God's mercy and justice, we act as if *we* are "laying down the law for God."

Jesus calms the storm

Of course, as Catholics, we have an even better image yet of how if we trust and hope in the One who is humble and gentle of heart, he will see us safely home to heaven through any earthly storms. (See Matthew 8:23–27; Mark 4:35–41; and Luke 8:22–25.)

Indeed, in a most poignant passage in her *Dialogues*, God tells St. Catherine of Siena that Judas' greatest sin was not his betrayal of Christ but his unwillingness to believe that God would forgive him had he asked.

So, as deadly serious as presumption and despair can be, we should always remember that hope can still defeat them, if we let it. If we have acted presumptuously or despairingly, we must remember that God will forgive any sin (even presumption or despair) if we humbly repent in our hearts and seek out the sacred remedy he has given us in the sacrament of Reconciliation.

Through humility we follow the laws that God laid down for us and thank him for giving us the highest of all hopes for a life of eternal happiness with him. We thank him as well for providing us with all the help we need to get there if we but follow his laws and accept his bountiful graces.

Dropping back down for the moment to the plane of natural hope, Thomas writes: "Love is caused by hope, and not vice versa. Because by the very fact that we hope that good will accrue to us through someone, we are moved towards him as to our own good; and thus we begin to love him."[97] Even more so does the supernatural virtue of hope flow into the greatest love of all, our love of God, caused by the love of God for us that he pours into our hearts and souls. So let's turn next to the virtue of love itself, the "mother of the virtues," and let's see how this great queen mother is attended by her handmaid of humility.

Humility Loves

The *Catechism* defines charity as "the theological virtue by which we love God above all things for his own sake, and our neighbor as ourselves for the love of God" (CCC 1822). St. Paul told us "If I ... have not love, I am nothing. If I ... have not love, I gain nothing" (1 Corinthians 13:2–3). Further: "So faith, hope, love abide, these three; but the greatest of these is love" (1 Corinthians 13:13). St. Thomas chimes in to call charity the "form" of the virtues, the "mother of the other virtues," and to say, "Charity is the friendship of man for God."[98]

Well, it doesn't get any better than this, and this is the powerful love and call to friendship God infuses into our hearts from the moment of our Baptism. Let's take a look now at what Paul calls *agape*, what Thomas calls *caritas*, and what we call *charity* or *love*, from a variety of angles— and through the lens of humility.

As to charity's relation to the other theological virtues, through *faith* we know God, though he is unseen; through *hope* we desire to see and be with him, and we trust in him to help us reach heaven; through *charity* we love God for his own sake and love others and ourselves through our love of him.[99]

Charity, Paul tells us, is the greatest of the three. It is also the only one that will last forever in heaven. We will no longer need faith when in heaven, since we will have no need to believe God regarding things not seen when we actually see them. Faith will be replaced by direct knowledge of God. Neither will we need to hope to live a life of bliss with God some day when we are eternally living it. Yet our love of God and of neighbor as ourselves will burn most intensely forever when we are actually united with God, the highest object of our love.

While charity alone endures forever in heaven, it also "quickens" as Thomas says, or brings alive and perfects our faith and hope while on earth. St. James tells us so clearly, "for as the body apart from the spirit is dead, so faith apart from works is dead" (James 2:26). He tells us that "even the demons believe—and shudder" (James 2:19).

Shuddering Demons Cast Out Humility and Love

Indeed, Satan and his minions certainly believe that God exists, but they do not love him, us, or ultimately even their own true selves. Because they lack love, their belief in God produces no good works. In a very real sense, charity is a virtue that works, a virtue that gets good things done, a virtue that the demons, through their explicit prideful rejection of God, have fired (so to speak) and banished from hell.

But let's think of it at an earthly level. Are we not willing to do and undertake the most arduous tasks for those we love most? Indeed, if any loving mother of an adult child were to look back at all the less-than-pleasant or difficult tasks she lovingly performed for her child, from diapers changed to wounds tended to advice dispensed to countless expenses gladly paid, she would agree that the more powerful is one's love, the more one is inspired and energized to get the jobs done! At a supernatural level, God's love for us is an infinitely greater power source for good.

The Big Furnace That Could

In one of my favorite insights on charity, St. Thomas makes a comparison between the love of charity and a hot furnace.[100] The more powerful the furnace, the more its heat will spread, even to our enemies. Indeed, "our love for God is proved to be so much the stronger, as the more difficult are the things we accomplish for its sake, just as the power of fire is so much the stronger, as it is able to set fire to a less inflammable matter."[101] And yet, just as those who are nearest the fire will be warmed the most, so too should the fires of our charity embrace with the greatest heat God himself, our Creator, and our family members and friends, as well as those living and working and worshipping near us.

As Thomas tells us, echoing Christ, our charity must include a love for *ourselves*, with our own bodies. Thomas notes that the natural love of self and desire for self-preservation that we all share forms the basis of natural friendship and love, whereby we proceed to treat others as we treat ourselves (as Christ explicitly bids us do—see Matthew 7:12).

While the theological virtue of charity is infused in our souls by God's love, and is therefore potentially unlimited in power, we are called to do our part too. The intensity of our fires of charity can grow or dwindle depending on how we act. Thomas tells us that each act of charity we perform strengthens our disposition or tendency to further acts of charity, "and this readiness increasing, man breaks out into an act of more fervent love, and strives to advance in charity, and then his charity increases actually."[102] As Aristotle says, we learn to construct a building or play an instrument through practice, and Thomas adds that we grow to love deeply through, indeed, practicing acts of love.

So, hopefully it is clear, even from a quick look at but a few of its facets, why charity resides at the pinnacle of our temple of virtue. Now let's look at its base once more to see a few ways how lowly humility helps lofty charity rise and remain at its heights.

Why We All Should Be Humbled by God's Loving Request

Have you ever heard someone say he or she was "humbled" by some kind of honor or award? Perhaps you have said so yourself? (I will admit *I* was humbled to even be considered for writing a book on humility of all things. Indeed, my wife could hardly believe it!) If we truly feel humbled by some honor we receive, perhaps a confidence that has been placed in us to perform some task or accolades given for some prior achievement, it does not necessarily mean that we deny our capacity and willingness to carry out the task, or declare that our achievement was not worthwhile. Rather, it expresses a desire to focus on the task or achievement itself and not just on one's self as the person who will or did accomplish it. Further, to truly feel humbled implies our recognition that few tasks are accomplished by our own efforts alone without the support of friends, family, coworkers, and of course, of God himself.

Your "Friend Request" from God Almighty: Confirm or Delete?

Now, let's consider that of all possible honors or awards to render us humble, none exceeds the *charity* God pours into our souls. When Thomas tells us "charity is the friendship of man for God" he built his insight upon the words of the Word of God himself: "No longer do I call you servants ... but I have called you friends" (John 15:15). St. Paul reiterates the point: "God is faithful, by whom you were called into the fellowship of his Son, Jesus Christ our Lord" (1 Corinthians 1:9). Indeed, Thomas shows in his treatise on *The Two Commandments of Charity* that God's love for us penetrates deeper still into our hearts. Not only does charity make us God's *friends* it also makes us his own *children:* "See what love the Father has given us, that we should be called children of God; and so we are" (1 John 3:1).

Almighty God's loving paternal friendship with us is truly the most humbling honor of all. Every time we prayerfully ponder this fact, it should lead us to a deeper *love of humility* and a deeper *love of love* itself. In the words of St. Augustine, "He that loves his neighbor, must, in consequence, love love itself."[103] Thomas elaborates, as we have seen, that charity is not only *love* but has the nature of *friendship* as well. In friendship we love the friend and wish him good things, and secondly, we love the good we wish for the friend. It is in this second way that we love charity out of charity, because charity is that good which we wish him. "Charity is itself the fellowship of the spiritual life, whereby we arrive at happiness."[104]

The unbeatable team of humility and charity will not only make us better friends to our close friends and neighbors (those closest to the furnace, as Thomas might say), but they will also make us more loving and friendly to every person we meet. And yet, their team cannot accomplish good works if they are shackled by *false* or *mistaken conceptions of humility*.

True Humility Extends a Hand to the Lonely

Scores of major psychological studies in recent years have documented rates of reported *loneliness* skyrocketing around the world (and this *before* the lockdowns and "social distancing" of 2020).[105] Well, for some lonely people, simple acts of acknowledgment—eye contact, a nod, a smile, a brief conversation, an invitation to go do something together—can mean the world to them.

Since studies around the world indicate around a third of the population may feel significantly lonely at any time, we are often around lonely people, whether we know it or not.[106] We should never hold back from reaching out to people in these simple ways because of a mistaken sense of humility, thinking, "Who am I that they should care whether I reach out to them or not?" True humility says, "I will reach out to them in love, even though they might well ignore or reject me." (After all, even the love Jesus offered to people on earth was often rejected.)

We know charity abides forever in heaven, and I imagine humility will too. For even those graced with glorified bodies someday will see how they pale in comparison to the unspeakable glory of God and will strive to use them to glorify him.

Humility's Holy Toolbox:

Unlocking Humility's Holy Toolbox for the Virtues of Loving

1. **Pray** to become more humbly receptive to the three theological virtues. Early in his comprehensive prayer "To Acquire the Virtues," St. Thomas writes: "O God ... Grant that I may abide on the firm ground of faith, be sheltered by an impregnable shield of hope, and be adorned in the bridal garment of charity."[107]

   The Church has also long prayed three simple prayers to obtain these virtues:[108]

   ### Act of Faith
   O my God, I firmly believe that you are one God in three divine Persons, Father, Son, and Holy Spirit. I believe that your divine Son became man and died for our sins and that he will come to judge the living and the dead. I believe these and all the truths which the Holy Catholic Church teaches because you have revealed them who are eternal truth and wisdom, who can neither deceive nor be deceived. In this faith I intend to live and die. Amen.

   ### Act of Hope
   O Lord God, I hope by your grace for the pardon of all my sins and after life here to gain eternal happiness because you have promised it who are infinitely powerful, faithful, kind, and merciful. In this hope I intend to live and die. Amen.

Act of Love

O Lord God, I love you above all things and I love my neighbor for your sake because you are the highest, infinite and perfect good, worthy of all my love. In this love I intend to live and die. Amen.

Alternatively, might you craft a simple prayer in your own words, or simply sit (or kneel) down and talk to God about them?

2. **Remember, I say, your Baptism day.** Now you may not be able to actually recall; after all, most of you were likely rather small. Still, there is no reason we cannot think back on a regular basis to the fact that we were baptized and filled with God's graces. (Sorry for sounding like Dr. Seuss, but a few too many pages on virtues and your brain gets loose.)

   Seriously though, while we formally reaffirm our baptismal vows at Easter Vigil or Easter Sunday Masses (vows originally professed by parents and godparents for most of us), we can certainly profit by reflecting back from time to time on what a wonderful gift our baptism was. It freed us from Satan's thrall and united us to the Body of Christ. It opened our souls to God's myriad graces and infused them with faith, hope, and charity. Baptism is the sacrament Church Fathers paired most closely with the virtue of faith itself. In Baptism, we all literally soaked in faith as a free gift of God, but it is up to us to make sure our souls do not dry out. We'll keep them lush and vibrant when watered every day with acts of faith, hope, charity—and Christian humility.

Chapter 3 Summary and Reflections

While all natural virtues are founded upon the base of humility, the supernatural, God-infused, theological virtues of faith, hope, and charity can build our spiritual temples all the way up to heaven. It takes humility to grasp both the power and the limitations of unaided human reason and to take a leap of faith whereby we *believe in God* and *believe God.*

It takes humility to keep from presuming we can get to heaven on our own, without embracing God's grace and his laws, and to keep from despairing of the power of God's justice and mercy, thinking that our own sinfulness is beyond God's power of forgiveness and love. It takes humility to stand in awe of the fact that through his unfathomable love, God, the Creator himself, has called us, his lowly creatures, to become his friends and adopted children and to share his love with all our neighbors. We might ask ourselves questions like these:

- In what *specific* ways can I heed the Church's call to train myself to live in humility today? How might I do this in simple acts or words in my interaction with my spouse, children, parents, coworkers, or neighbors?

- Am I training myself *daily* through prayer and Bible reading to take farther and higher leaps of faith, to know God better, to believe him more deeply, to trust in him and love him more fully? (Or, if you might prefer a more eloquent rendering, here is one version of the beautiful words St. Richard of Chichester prayed to God: "May I know thee more clearly, love thee more dearly, and follow thee more nearly, day by day.")[109]

- Have I embraced the virtue of hope within my soul, so that my thoughts, words, and deeds serve the great end God has set before me of a life of bliss with him, and have I shared the joy of my hope with my loved ones?

- Have I been humbled by God's invitation to be his friend and his child? Have I accepted it wholeheartedly? Have I recognized fully that he has extended this invitation to everyone around me and that I should treat *them* as the friends, sons, and daughters of God?

Humility Lived Saint Story #3

Blessed Pier Giorgio Frassati (1901–1925)

The pawn ticket belongs to Sappa; I had forgotten it. Please renew it on my account.[110]

–Blessed Pier Giorgio Frassati

Handsome, athletic, vivacious, wealthy, and ever popular with his peers—a life of humility might have come hard to the young son of the eminent Alfredo Frassati, owner and chief editor of Italy's prominent newspaper *La Stampa* and Italy's ambassador to Germany, had he not so embraced the virtues of faith, hope, and charity.

Young Pier Giorgio took great joy in life. He loved to belt out the joyous, boisterous operas of Giuseppe Verdi (even if a bit off key) and to recite loudly outdoors the sonorous Italian poetry of Dante. Indeed, neighbors called it his "preaching." One of his favorite activities was hiking together with his good friends. High in the mountains, he not only gazed at the vistas and thanked God for the beauty but also, at times, attended Mass in alpine chapels.

Though their activities were virtuous, his tight-knit group of friends humorously dubbed themselves *Tipi Loschi*, the "Sinister Ones" or "Shady Characters." In truth, Pier Giorgio's humble, loving character spread the golden light of God's love like few others.

As a teenager, he saw the need to strive to promote social change, and he became active in the Italian Catholic Youth Society and in the Federation of Catholic University students, but he never forgot the well-being of those close to him, as well.

Pier was constantly giving alms and assistance to the poor. When asked by friends why he, a wealthy young man, always rode trains in third class, he said it was because there was no fourth class! (Talk about poverty of spirit!) Similarly, when some would drive or ride trains to meetings far away, Pier Giorgio often arrived sweaty, traveling by bicycle so he could give his train fare to the poor.

His sister has provided a particularly wonderful glimpse into his character, so founded in humility and fired by Christian charity. Whenever he entered a crowded room, he would look around for the most forlorn, out of place, or lonely looking person and proceed to spend time chatting with that person.

Pier Giorgio's brief life had a tragic ending—by worldly standards anyway. Though his family did not know it until his condition had progressed almost to its end, Pier Giorgio was struck by an illness that paralyzed his legs. Once he was examined by a doctor, it became clear that he had a rare form of poliomyelitis, which he likely caught from ministering to the sick. No treatment could be found in Italy. Realizing he did not have long to live, Pier Giorgio wrote a note for a friend from the St. Vincent de Paul Society, the one in our Saint Story heading. It read, in part, "The pawn ticket belongs to Sappa; I had forgotten it. Please renew it on my account."

Though dying, Pier Giorgio was thinking of others. Not just at the last but throughout his life, he lived out the words of St. John, in imitation of Christ: "Greater love has no man than this, that a man lay down his life for his friends" (John 15:13).

Blessed Pier Giorgio Frassati, pray for us, that we may grow in the kind of humility and love that brings us joy in this life and helps spread it to all around us, until the day we all gather to sing out loudly (even if a bit off key), above the highest of mountains, in the choirs of *Paradiso*.[111]

PART II

Humility Battles Sins

Recollect yourself now interiorly, and examine yourself,
and having found that under one or other of these headings,
pride really dominates you, judge how necessary it is for you
to fight against it with humility, because if pride is conquered,
a host of other sins will be conquered also.[112]

—Fr. Cajetan Mary da Bergamo

OK. So our humility assembly manual is certainly loaded with parts, but hopefully by now we have identified them and realized that God has made them available for every one of us. Now it is time to move from the "Parts" section to the "Warnings!" (and from a mechanical metaphor to a biological one).

Not only does humility provide the fertile soil from which all the virtues grow, it helps every one of these virtues uproot the noxious weeds of the opposing vices that may grow in our souls. Indeed, the most noxious weed of all is *pride*, the antithesis of humility. In the chapter that follows we will see how humility can help us overcome the seven deadly sins in all of their noxious varieties, their forty-four "death-dealing daughters," and the "queen of the vices" that spawns them all.

So let's get ready to stand firmly upon the solid ground of humility and don "the whole armor of God," from "the belt of truth" to "the breastplate of righteousness," our feet shod "with the equipment of the gospel of peace ... taking the shield of faith ... the helmet of salvation, and the sword of the Spirit, which is the word of God" (Ephesians 6:13–17), and prepare to do spiritual battle with pride and its host of minions.

The sins to follow can indeed be deadly to our souls. With humility at our side, although we might end up with some scrapes and bruises now and then, we will always survive them and come through spiritually stronger than before we got close enough to take a good look at them.

Chapter 4

HUMILITY CONQUERS
THE SEVEN DEADLY SINS

For the tempting vices, which fight against us in invisible contest in behalf of the pride which reigns over them, some of them go first, like captains, others follow, after the manner of an army. For all faults do not occupy the heart with equal access. But while the greater and the few surprise a neglected mind, the smaller and the numberless pour themselves upon it in a whole body.[113]

—St. Gregory the Great

While the individual sins that have become known across the centuries as the seven deadly sins or seven capital sins (or vices) appear many hundreds of times in Scripture, they do not appear all together in a list in any particular verse. They are listed clearly in the *Catechism* though: "They are pride, avarice, envy, wrath, lust, gluttony, and sloth or acedia" (CCC 1866).

So where does this list come from? The *Catechism* notes that St. John Cassian (AD 360–435) and St. Gregory the Great (c. AD 540–604) played important roles in developing it. Indeed, the story of the Church's teaching on the seven deadly sins is a fascinating one. It builds upon the wisdom of many other Eastern and Western Church Fathers and Doctors on down to our own St. Thomas Aquinas.

We will encounter some of these and other key figures in this chapter, but our focus will here be squarely upon how humility can help us conquer this *seven-headed* (or perhaps *eight-headed* as you will soon see) monster of sin that seeks to destroy every one of us.

Humility Slays a Seven-Headed Dragon

Before we begin, please note that these sins are called deadly sins because they can lead us to mortal sins that spell the death of our souls. They are also called capital sins (the *Catechism* uses this wording), taking their name from the Latin word *caput*, "head." The word "head" here is used in a metaphorical sense, just as we call a CEO or pastor the "head" of a business or parish.

The Horse That Sniffed Sin

In explaining the seven capital sins, St. Gregory the Great starts by citing Job 39:25: "When the trumpet sounds, he says, 'Aha!' He smells the battle from afar, the thunder of the captains, and the shouting." Taking this picture of the warhorse ready to do battle, Gregory then explains this verse in moral terms to help us understand the capital sins. He speaks as if the seven deadly sins are leaders of a mighty, lethal enemy force made up of an array of sins. So let's look at these deadly leaders one by one and find out how lowly humility can unseat them from their high horses.

Humility Guts Gluttony

I would not be surprised if you (like me) have not heard a homily on *gluttony* in awhile—or have not brought it up in confession. Surely, we have more serious things to worry about than eating too much! "On the contrary, Gregory says (Moral. xxx, 18) that 'unless we first tame the enemy dwelling within us, namely our gluttonous appetite, we have not even stood up to engage in the spiritual combat.'"[114]

St. Gregory opines to the contrary (and St. Thomas nods in agreement) because gluttony can serve as what we might call a "gateway" sin, a sin that if left unchecked can open the door to all kinds of other sins. Gluttony is the first of the two deadly sins that deal directly with things of the body, the other being *lust*. Gregory and other Church Fathers noted that if we do not train ourselves to rein in inappropriate desires for food and drink, we will be far less likely to rein in our appetites for inappropriate sexual activities as well.

Combating gluttony is great training in battling lust, the other bodily deadly sin, because we get opportunities to practice eating and drinking properly several times through the course of every day to build up the virtue of temperance in our souls. If we do not even try to do this, to paraphrase Gregory, we have not even stood up from the table to engage in spiritual combat!

Beware Mad Gut Disease

Still, to understand the nature of gluttony, we need to understand that it certainly means more than simply eating too much. I love the ancient Greek Fathers' word for gluttony—*gastrimargia*, meaning a "madness of the gut or the stomach"!

When St. Gregory and St. Thomas Aquinas expound upon the "varieties" of the sin of gluttony, they defined gluttony as *an inordinate or irrational desire for food* and described dangers of eating too much food, too-expensive food, or too-daintily-prepared food, and of eating too quickly or eating too often. In the thirteenth century, St. Thomas cites an old medieval verse that summed up the various forms in which gluttonous behaviors are expressed "hastily, sumptuously, too much, greedily, daintily."[115]

It is through this more nuanced understanding of gluttony that we can better examine our own consciences to see if this vice is weighing down our souls (and maddening our bellies) and to understand how humility can help us rein it in. We saw that Thomas examines the virtue of humility in terms of its close relationship to the cardinal virtue of *temperance.* Humility's job is to help temperance rein in inordinate hopes or desires, and its job duties can extend to hopes and desires for things as ostensibly mundane as food.

Humility champions temperance and knows that "enough is as good as a feast." (Indeed, it is probably better!) Still, humility's role might jump out most clearly in the varieties of gluttony that demand only expensive or daintily prepared food, since that kind of gluttony says, "The simple, plain foods of the earth are simply not good enough for *me!*" This does not mean that we should not appreciate fine foods or even develop gourmet skills to make them, but it means that when provided with simpler fare we show gratitude for that food as well, knowing perfectly well it is plenty good enough for us.

Humility extends to all of the varieties of gluttony, from wolfing down our food to eating around the clock, by putting our desires for good into context, enabling us to desire to eat to live rather than to live to eat. It reminds us that God crafted our bodies from the earth and designed them so that, while on earth and before we receive our glorified bodies in heaven, we should need to keep supplying them in proper proportions with the earth's edible bounty. And in that regard, humility remembers we are called to treat our bodies as temples of the Holy Spirit (see 1 Corinthians 6)—and not oversupply warehouses!

I should give one caveat before we move on. Gluttony is certainly more than skin deep, and you cannot always determine its presence by placing someone on a scale. Some inherit genetic tendencies to weigh more than others and may do so even with quite moderate eating habits. Surely you know as well some people who seem to have a hollow leg and can eat a great deal while staying slim. Remember, the key aspect to gluttony is an inordinate or irrational desire for food. Indeed, I can hardly think of any times I have had more inordinate and irrational desires for food than many decades ago when *dieting* excessively for a bodybuilding contest. It was hard to think of much else than what was on the menu for my next meal, not the best state of mind to embrace humility or engage in spiritual combat!

Humility Tempers Lust

The next carnal or bodily sin among the seven deadly sins is lust, "disordered desire for or inordinate enjoyment of sexual pleasure," as the *Catechism* tells us (CCC 2351). Like gluttony, lust is a perversion or corruption of something naturally good and essential to human life. We cannot live as individuals without food, of course, and we cannot carry on as a species without sexual union. Since the Fall of Adam and Eve, lust, though not the worst of sins compared to some spiritual sins, has been perhaps the most tempting, and one that can lead to devastating consequences.

As to its vehemence, Church Fathers such as St. Thomas and St. Augustine note that lust arises from *concupiscence*, a powerful desire arising from our lower sensual appetites that is contrary to right reason, and as most of us can probably attest from lived experience, it is difficult for reason to control.

As for lust's potentially dire consequences if it is not constrained, consider how it has led in our time to everything from the proliferation of pornography to increasing cases of adultery and divorce and, proving it can truly be a "deadly" sin, to more than seventy million abortions worldwide every year.[116] Indeed, when I have given talks on the seven deadly sins to Catholic audiences and asked for a show of hands regarding which sin members of the audience think is causing the most havoc in our world today, *lust wins hands up, every time.*

An Argument in Which the Devil Will Defeat You

Temperance is the cardinal virtue that specifically counters lust. It is assisted by specific moral virtues like *chastity*, which guides proper use of our sexuality or celibacy for those who are married or single. Still, these virtues can use every bit of help from other virtues, too, foremost among them humility. St. John Climacus makes this crystal clear:

> Do not imagine that you will overwhelm the demon of fornication by entering into an argument with him. Nature is on his side and he has the best of the argument. So the man who decides to struggle against his flesh and to overcome it by his own efforts is fighting in vain. The truth is

that unless the Lord overturns the house of the flesh and builds the house of the soul, the man wishing to overcome it has watched and fasted for nothing. Offer up to the Lord the weakness of your nature. Admit your incapacity and, without your knowing it, you will win for yourself the gift of chastity.[117]

True humility can conquer lust by helping us see the truth about the limited power of our reason and will and calling upon the unlimited power of God's grace, through prayer and confession—again and again, if necessary. Indeed, St. John Climacus tells us that trying to conquer lust without humbly requesting God's grace is like swimming across the sea with one hand tied behind our backs.[118]

Humility Abolishes Avarice

St. Thomas said that the sin of *avarice* or greed most directly opposes the virtue of justice. Justice gives to each person his or her rightful due, while avarice says, "I deserve more!"

Thomas calls avarice the "immoderate love of possessing."[119] We could say that those most deeply mired in greed are "possessed with possessing."

Like lust and greed, avarice too is a perversion of something good, since it is a good thing to work and acquire money to meet our needs and the needs of our families, our church, and other worthy causes. Still, avarice, like lust, is a very powerful drive for some.

Thomas clarifies that while Scripture says that "love of money is the root of all evils; it is through this craving that some have wandered away from the faith and pierced their hearts with many pangs" (1 Timothy 6:10), this verse does not say money itself but "love of money" is the root of evils. Further, this does not mean that avarice causes every other sin. St. Paul elaborates within the same verse that "some" have lost their faith and suffer from it. Rather, an inordinate love of money acts like a root.

Avarice drives a person to pursue wealth, and that wealth can facilitate his or her quest to commit other sins. As St. Thomas explains, this makes avarice like the roots of a poisonous plant that draw nutrients out of the soil so the plant can grow taller and stronger. Certainly, sins like gluttony can be roots in their turn, giving rise to avarice itself, so avarice is by no means the only sin that can be the source of other evils. Still, avarice is more often behind other sins, since it can serve as the means to many mean ends.

How do we know if avarice has us in its greedy clutches? We can examine our consciences to see if we are excessively concerned about money and the things it can buy. Are we constantly thinking of ways to earn more money? Are we driven to work second jobs or to take advantage of every possible overtime hour? We really need to consider if, at the end of our lives, we will wish we spent more time at the office and less with our families and friends.

We can also look at what St. Gregory and St. Thomas calls the "daughters" of avarice. Every deadly sin spawns other sins that serve it or express it. They called them "daughters" to stress their ability to give birth to related sins.[120]

As for avarice, the daughters born of it are a sorry lot indeed—*treachery, fraud, falsehood, perjury*, and *violence*. Hopefully most of us have no room to house such heinous and criminal daughters in our souls. (Or if we have, we have confessed them and made sincere amends.)

The first of the daughters of avarice we have more likely rented space to in our souls is *restlessness*. Can we never rest satisfied, always desiring more—more money or more goods that money can buy? As the Stoic philosopher Seneca put it so pithily, "It is not the man who has little who is poor, but the one who hankers after more."[121] Are we always hankering?

The second of greed's daughters we might have let in is called *insensitivity to mercy*. It is an *illiberality* that opposes the virtue of liberality we mentioned in chapter 2—the willingness to give freely from our surplus to people who are in need. It is the daughter embraced by the tightwad, the skinflint, the Scrooge before the Spirits of Christmas helped free him from greed's miserly clutches.

But what has *humility* to do with avarice? For one thing, humility remembers the only thing that will put our restlessness to rest. Augustine said our hearts are restless until they rest in God. Before him, Christ said, "Come to me, all who labor and are heavy laden, and I will give you rest"

(Matthew 11:28). Humility recognizes that we are meant to labor, but the money it brings will never bring rest to our souls. It is *poverty of spirit* that will earn us the kingdom of heaven (see Matthew 5:3). And even while here on earth, in the words of the Catholic poet Prudentius, "'Tis the deepest of rest to wish for nought beyond what due need calls for."[122]

Humility Routs Wrath

Thomas notes that anger is a natural human passion that may or may not be expressed appropriately. Building on Aristotle's insights, Thomas notes that for our anger not to be sinful, it must be aimed at the correct person (someone who is actually at fault), expressed at the correct time (not at once but when some time has passed, so our passion of anger cools and is tempered), and oriented toward the correct goal (to correct, not to injure the wrongdoer, or to protect society).

The Latin word for wrath is *ira*, and even in English, to raise someone's ire means to arouse their anger. As I have written elsewhere,

> *wrath*, or excessive anger, is also a very powerful and deadly sin, because it, like lust, builds on a natural sensitive passion hardwired into our fallen human nature. Whereas lust is a failure of our reason to rein in our concupiscible appetite for things that we desire, wrath is a failure of our reason to rein in our irascible appetite that seeks to fight back against things that thwart our desires. "Nature does nothing without a purpose," per Aristotle. Our concupiscible, fleshly desires ensure the propagation of our species, and those irascible, fight-or-flight responses ensure our safety and survival. We've seen as well that part of the reason the seven capital vices are so deadly is that they seek out things that seem good to us, and when we have chosen the wrong goods to seek, we let loose legions of sinful behaviors that serve these ill-chosen ends. [123]

So let's take a quick look at how wrath does this and at how lowly humility can lower its ire.

There are many ways we can be wrathful. For example, consider the irritable person who flies off the handle at the slightest of inconveniences. You may have encountered him "road raging" on the highway or cursing the kitchen cabinet that dared to jump out and strike her in the head. (Or maybe, like me, you have even acted like that a time or two!)

The sullen person, though, may not lash out all of a sudden but will quietly nurse old wounds, refusing to forgive, forget, or let them go, perhaps even savoring the warmth of their smoldering anger, keeping hot the fires within their hearts until the perfect opportunity for revenge should arise. In modern psychological lingo, some speak of the sullen as passive–aggressive personalities.

Those called rancorous or ill-tempered refuse to apologize or even let up on their anger, even after they have lashed out at someone through some unjust act of vengeance or retribution, and even if their target was a loved one.

All forms of wrath have in common that they are, in the words of Seneca, who wrote a book on anger (*De ira*), "temporary madness." He also said the following: "But anger may be routed by precepts; for it is a weakness of the mind that is subject to the will."[124]

Humility, we have seen, is devoted to grasping the *truth*, which is the opposite of madness. Humility will seek out and remind us of truths that we may use as "precepts" to route our anger, reel us back from the brink of madness, and bring our heated emotions under the cool control of our intellect and will. The humble can learn and train themselves in truthful self-statements to use when they feel wrath beginning to simmer within.

Wrath says, "How dare you insult or harm me! I will get even, sooner or later." Humility says, "I am no special case. I'm as prone to insult and injury as anyone else. I will try to understand how your behavior toward me somehow made sense to you. If I am in a position to correct you somehow, I will do it with your best interest in mind. If I'm in no such position, I'll endure it and move on!"

Further, humility can prepare us in advance for anger-provoking situations we might find ourselves facing any day. The Stoic philosopher-emperor Marcus Aurelius recommended a mental morning exercise in which we prepare ourselves to come in contact that day with "the busybody, the thankless, the overbearing, the treacherous, the envious, the unneighborly."[125] (Unfortunately, the seven deadly sins are alive and well today, just as they were in the time of Marcus Aurelius.)

Far from hating such people, Aurelius urged that we ought to see them as brothers whom we can learn to work with. Indeed, the reason that they behave as they do is their failure to genuinely grasp goodness. Comprehending what is good on our part will help us recognize that they are human, just like us, and that *their* behavior cannot drag down *our* souls. The Stoic emperor's advice can help us Christians today to grow in humility and avoid wrath if we take his words to heart each day!

Humility Slashes Sloth
(That Can Move Quite Quickly If It Wants To)

Sloth means far more than lazily crunching chips on the couch in front of the TV, patiently waiting for your wife to arise so you can ask, "Honey, would you please bring me a drink—while you're up?" Sloth may connote a general laziness to many people, especially if you ever watched a slow-motion sloth in a zoo. It may seem a most unlikely candidate for a list of deadly sins.

How odd then that St. Thomas would consider it a sin that directly opposes what Christ named as the greatest commandment of all—to "love the Lord your God with all your heart, and with all your soul, and with all your mind, and with all your strength" (Mark 12:30; see Matthew 22:37; Luke 10:27; Deuteronomy 6:5).

Perhaps you noticed that the *Catechism* calls this sin "sloth or acedia" (CCC 1866). In his *Summa Theologica*, Thomas used the Latin word *acedia*, the Latinized version of the Greek word *akedeia*, which literally means "without care." The deadly sin of sloth or acedia (or *akedeia* if you prefer), is a *spiritual apathy*, a *boredom or sadness about the things of God.* Do you see now how sloth or acedia is diametrically opposed to loving God with every fiber of our being?

If we are mired in such spiritual apathy, we may well be quite physically lazy too—regarding the things that show our love of God, things like prayer and going to Mass. Still, the person mired in sloth might seem anything but lazy in other areas of his life. Thomas noted that the minds of people who take no joy in spiritual things will go "wandering ... after unlawful things,"[126] snared by one of sloth's deadly daughters. Even the pagan Aristotle knew well that "those who find no joy in spiritual pleasures, have recourse to pleasures of the body."[127] So, the minds and the bodies of the slothful may remain active seeking things they should not be seeking, or excessively seeking out lesser goods. The frenzied workaholic or exercise fanatic who has no time for Mass may well be a model of slothful behavior.

We have seen that the sin of sloth or acedia is a disregard of God. Acedia says in words and deeds (or the lack thereof), "God, I do not care!" So how can humility help us avoid sloth? Well, we saw in chapter 1 that St. Thomas said, "Humility, considered as a special virtue, regards chiefly the subjection of man to God."[128] This is how humility slashes sloth. When we humbly subject ourselves to God, we will think about our love for him and strive to remember and serve him with all of the powers and gifts he has given us. Humility says, "God, I care about you above all else," and, if we have lapsed into sloth or any other sin, it says by its words and its actions within the confessional booth, "Oh my God, I am heartily sorry for having offended you."

Humility Ends Envy

Envy is as deadly as ever in our day, and it can operate at both the individual and societal levels. St. Thomas notes that while sloth directly opposes the greatest commandment, envy directly opposes the second great commandment that follows it: "You shall love your neighbor as yourself" (Mark 12:31; see Matthew 22:39; Luke 10:27). We speak of being "green with envy" because it can be very unpleasant to experience it, making us green at the gills, so to speak, the color that Thomas suggests might be blue. The deadly sin of envy is a *sadness* we experience in response to someone else's good.

We often speak of jealousy and envy interchangeably, but while jealousy makes us sad when we might lose something we have that is good (think of the jealous spouse), envy is the disturbance we experience when *somebody else has something good.* Indeed, the envious might not even want what the other person has, he simply does not want him to have it! Most serious is the envy of another person's *spiritual* good, perhaps due to the fact that a sinner has converted to Christ and now receives positive attention for mending his ways and performing charitable acts. We always want goods for ourselves, and most of all our eternal salvation. If we are to love others *as ourselves*, we can see how clearly envy contradicts that obligation.

The Tales of Envy's Five Green and Blue Daughters

St. Thomas has laid out envy's daughters in an interesting sequence, so let's take a quick look at envy's brood in action (and see if we see ourselves in any of them).

- Have we practiced *tale-bearing*, spreading malicious gossip behind the back of a person we envy to bring him down a notch or two in the eyes of others?

- Have we practiced *detraction*, wherein face-to-face with the person we envy we banter with her in a way that belittles the good that has come her way, perhaps by pretending to praise it but actually putting it down or comparing it to someone else's greater accomplishment?

- If we have managed to make the person we envy look small, do we *enjoy that person's discomfort*, falling prey to another of envy's petty daughters?

- In the event that our envious efforts have not succeeded, do we feel *sad* that we were unable to spoil our neighbor's good?

- Such a sequence of thoughts, emotions, words, and deeds builds up to an ugly climax. The final sinful daughter of envy is *hatred*, an evil that is clearly the opposite of the call to charity.

- St. Paul knew well humility's power over envy when he advised us, "In humility count others better than yourselves" (Philippians 2:3). *Envy* says, "That person's happiness makes me sad. He does not deserve it like I do." *Humility* says, "Good for him for successfully employing his God-given talents! Since I love him like I love myself, his happiness increases mine."

Venerable Louis of Grenada (1505–1588) summed up this sentiment most eloquently:

When you envy the virtue of another you are your own greatest enemy; for if you continue in a state of grace, united to your neighbor through charity, you have a share in all his good works, and the more he merits the richer you become. So far, therefore, from envying his virtue, you should find it a source of consolation. Alas! Because your neighbor is advancing, will you fall back? Ah! If you would love in him the virtues which you do not find in yourself, you would share in them through charity; the profit of his labors would also become yours.[129]

Humility Vanquishes Vainglory

Here we are at deadly sin number seven, and we find *vainglory* waiting to show itself off for us. What happened to pride, you might ask? Don't worry, pride does take pride of place among the deadly sins, and we will turn to it next. Know for now, though, that in the sixth century, St. Gregory the Great formulated his list of the seven deadly sins, and it would prove foundational for the Church. His list did not include pride but did include *vana gloria* (vainglory). Seven centuries later St. Thomas followed suit. Let's take a look at vainglory now in all of its inane, humility-lacking splendor.

St. Thomas tells us that honor can be empty in three ways. First, one might desire to be praised for something vain or unimportant. Second, one might look for applause from people who are deficient in discernment. Or, third, one might be seeking glory to puff oneself up rather than to glorify God or do good to the souls of others.[130] To sum up, desiring honors for the *wrong things*, from the *wrong people*, or for the *wrong reasons* spells vainglory.

Three centuries later, St. Francis de Sales added some eloquent insights of his own:

> Vainglory is the glory that we give ourselves; either for what is not really in us, or for what is in fact in us but not owing to anything we did, or for what is in us and owing to us but which does not deserve to be the cause of a boast ... There are those who are proud and haughty because they ride a magnificent horse or because their hat sports a fancy feather, or because they are wearing some fashionable clothing. Who does not see the folly here? If there is glory due, it belongs to the horse, the bird or the tailor! And what a pitiable heart is his who expects esteem because of a horse, a feather or some lace![131]

As St. Francis tells us, if we look for applause because of actions or qualities we can't truly claim as our own or for things that should not "be the cause of a boast," we are falling prey to vainglory.

Clearly, vainglory is an affront to humility, since it says, "Look at me and how wonderful I am!" for things that are petty or for truly good things for which we fail to give God the credit and the glory that is his due. Consider how so often our modern popular culture in entertainment and sports glorifies celebrities for audacious and vulgar braggadocio. Consider too how some people are said to be "famous for being famous" with no significant positive achievements. How sad too that so many of us know far more about a panoply of celebrities than about the vast, humble communion of saints.

One good way to vanquish vainglory, however paradoxical this might sound, is to take a good long look in the mirror! I'm speaking metaphorically, of course, about a good examination of one's conscience. We might say something to ourselves like the following: "Mirror, mirror on the wall, is my soul the fairest of them all, or has it become blemished by thoughts, words, and deeds like these?"

- Do I look for applause because of the way I look or the things I have inherited? Do I show off my possessions or connections? After all, the One ultimately responsible for these blessings is God, and I ought to use them for his glory.

- Do I refuse to acknowledge when others show me where I'm mistaken in my thinking? Do I insist on being right even when I'm wrong? If so, vainglory's daughters of *obstinacy* and *discord* may have taken root in my soul. If I pick fights and demand that my preferences rule the day then I am being *contentious*, too.

- Do I draw attention to what I have by *boasting*?

- Do I follow the law and accept instructions from my superiors, or do I claim that my way is best, letting *disobedience* rear its head?

Vainglory says, "Look at glorious me!" Humility replies, "For the greater glory of God" (*ad majorem Dei gloriam*, the motto of the Jesuits)!

Seven Sinful Pronouncements
and Half a Dozen (plus one) Humble Rejoinders

Sin Declares:	Humility Responds:
Gluttony: "I deserve the largest quantities of the very best foods, prepared just the way I like them, and I deserve them now!"	"Bless us, O Lord, and these thy gifts we are about to receive (however plain and simple they might be) from thy bounty. Through Christ our Lord. Amen."
Lust: "That person's body is attractive to me. I must work to get it or, if that's not possible, at least think about it!"	"That person's body is indeed beautiful, but it also houses a soul. That person is someone's child, perhaps someone's sibling or parent. Someday, too, that body, like mine, will return to the soil from which it came. Thank you, Lord, for making our bodies beautiful in life. Please continue to shower that person with your blessings. Now, help me think about other things!"
Avarice: "Greed is good!"	"Enough is better than a fortune."
Wrath: "How dare that person insult or injure ME!"	"Who am I that I cannot be insulted or injured? Somehow that person's actions made sense to him or her. I'll speak up, if possible, but will certainly pray to God that he will soften that person's heart."
Sloth: "God, I don't care!"	"O my God, I am heartily sorry for having offended you ..."

Envy: "How dare another person have some good thing that I do not!"	"He or she is a child of God just as I am. As a fellow member of Christ's body joined in the bonds of charity, I say, Thanks be to God! And please keep the blessings headed their way!"
Vainglory: "Look at me and be thankful for your chance to gaze upon my awesomeness!	"If I've achieved anything noteworthy, to God be the glory and honor!"

Humility Conquers the "Queen of the Vices"

Aurelius Prudentius Clemens (c. AD 348–413) was inspired by classical battle epics like Homer's *Iliad* and Virgil's *Aeneid*. Building upon the story of Abraham's battle to win back his nephew Lot from his captivity at the hands of Mesopotamian kings (see Genesis 14), Prudentius wrote the allegorical poetic epic *Psychomachia* (or the *Fight for Mansoul*) in which he describes a graphic, bloody battle between virtues and vices.

In one of the most crucial battles, Pride, described as a warrior on horseback "galloping about, all puffed up,"[132] contemptuously dismisses the virtue of Lowliness. But Lowliness, allied with Hope, wins the day when Pride gallops headlong into a trap dug by Deceit, her comrade in arms, to ensnare their foes. As Scripture tells us, "Pride goes before destruction, and a haughty spirit before a fall" (Proverbs 16:18).

So here in this fictional tale we see lowly humility humbling haughty pride, assisted, as is fitting, by a theological virtue (hope) infused in lowly souls through the grace of God almighty. It works this way in real life too.

In his *Summa Theologica*, St. Thomas addresses pride in depth right after he examines humility, its direct contrary and most powerful enemy. But why did he not list pride among the seven deadly sins?

Good questions! Thomas, following St. Gregory the Great, considered pride the deadliest of all the sins and the most powerful source from which even the seven deadly sins flow. Indeed, they called pride the "queen of the vices." As I have written elsewhere,

> All sins involve a turning toward some lesser good or pleasure, while turning away from higher goods and, ultimately, from God. Some sins may be committed through ignorance or weakness, and may not be directly intended as affronts to God. Pride does not necessarily engender every sin one commits, but it has the potential to spawn every form of sin. A person may have serious problems with lust or with wrath, for example, but realize they offend God and strive mightily to conquer them. A person filled with the vice of pride may feel no compunction and openly defy God in his sinful acts. The word for pride in Latin is *superbia*, and Thomas says it "is so-called because a man thereby aims higher (*supra*) than he is." Pride is an inordinate desire for one's own excellence and to have things one's own way, rather than God's way ...
>
> Any of the seven deadly sins becomes far more deadly when openly flaunted through pride. Pride is also especially deadly because even the *virtues* that we develop may be kindling for its fires ...
>
> We must exercise special care, even as we pursue virtue, so that we do not fail to acknowledge our gratitude to God for whatever success we may achieve. Pride may lurk within even apparently quite saintly souls, and we must all exercise care that it does not lead us to a fall.[133]

Humility, then, is the virtue diametrically opposed to pride. It fights against pride in every form. It grounds us, helping us so that we never forget our God-given origin and identity. And while humility teams up with *hope* to defeat pride and deceit in Prudentius' imaginary battle for the human soul, humility's most powerful partner of all is the "mother of the virtues," the greatest theological virtue, the one that abides, the one that rests atop of the temple of virtue—namely, *charity.*

With humility at our holy temple's base, charity at its pinnacle, and all other virtues stacked up solidly in between, pride, its seven deadly sins, and all of their various death-dealing daughters can huff and puff until they run out of wind, but they'll never blow virtue's house down!

Humility's Holy Toolbox:

Supernatural Sin Squashers

1. **Prayer –** Wouldn't it be nice if we had a good prayer to help us avoid future sins? And how grand would it be if the prayer was as simple as it is profound? And for the icing on the prayer cake, imagine if this prayer was given to us by God himself?

    Thankfully, we have this prayer. Christ gave us the Our Father, as we read in Matthew 6:9–13. This prayer is so rich in meaning that many great theologians have analyzed it and found multiple insights within its every word. Since our chapter focused on humility as a means to route sins, I offer this simple table below to suggest some ways the Our Father can be seen to combat all seven deadly sins (and the "queen of the vices" who rules over them all):

Parts of the Lord's Prayer   **Opposing Deadly Sins**

Parts of the Lord's Prayer	Opposing Deadly Sins
1. Our Father,	1. Envy
2. who art in heaven,	2. Sloth
3. hallowed by thy name;	3. Vainglory
4. thy kingdom come, thy will be done, on earth as it is in heaven.	4. Pride
5. Give us this day our daily bread,	5. Gluttony, Avarice
6. and forgive us our trespasses as we forgive those who trespass against us;	6. Wrath
7. and lead us not into temptation,	7. Lust
8. but deliver us from evil. Amen."	8. All the deadly sins

✝ *Our Father"* – We pray to "our" Father, not "my" Father. This is a remedy for envy, which is self-absorbed and saddened by another's good, since it reminds us we are all members of the same family, brothers and sisters of the same loving Father, and we pray for the benefit of all.

✝ *"who art in heaven"* – This is a remedy for sloth, which is mired in earthly concerns, neglecting heavenly things and the holiness of God.

✝ *"hallowed be thy name"* – This is a remedy for vainglory, in which we seek earthly glory for our own names and neglect the honor due God.

✝ *"thy kingdom come, thy will be done, on earth as it is in heaven"* – This is a remedy for pride, that font from which all the deadly sins flow, in which our will and desires come first.

✝ *"Give us this day our daily bread"* – This is a remedy both for gluttony, which seeks more than a day's worth of bread at a time, and for avarice, which seeks more than one's share of any earthly goods. It is also as a reminder of the greatest of all breads, which we receive in the Eucharist.

✝ *"and forgive us our trespasses as we forgive those who trespass against us"* – This is a remedy against the unforgiving anger of wrath.

✝ *"and lead us not into temptation, but deliver us from evil"* – This is a remedy against the temptations of lust, the most powerful carnal temptations of all, as well as every kind of evil that comes from deadly sins.

Amen![134]

2. **The sacrament of Reconciliation** – This sacrament
   is called Reconciliation for good reason. St. Thomas
   says three key elements to this sacrament, also
   called the sacrament of Penance, are contrition,
   confession, and satisfaction.

   We must be contrite and truly regret our sins, confess
   them aloud to the priest, and atone or "make
   satisfaction" for our sins by carrying out the specific
   acts of penance the priest prescribes.

   Well, not only does this sacrament cleanse us of
   our sins, but it does indeed reconcile us to God and
   reopen his bountiful graces which we choose to close
   off by committing mortal sins. If we seek to grow in
   humility, we must remember that no matter how
   often we fall by rejecting God's helping hand, if we
   avail ourselves of the sacrament of Reconciliation,
   God is always fully willing to put us back on track.

Chapter 4 Summary and Reflections

Aristotle said that just as there are many ways an arrow can miss a target's bull's-eye, there are many vices that miss the target of virtue. This seems especially true of our bull's-eye of humility, since even *virtues* can make us miss if we think too much of ourselves for adding them to our quivers!

We can be thankful, however, that God gave us the Church and so many insightful saints to fully arm us and help us with effective target practice. It is an act of humility to acquire the habit of sincerely examining our consciences for the presence of pride and all the deadly sins, in all of their varieties and through all of their daughters. We can train ourselves to do this every day, and especially on days before we go to confession.

A Personal Reflection: How Pride and Vainglory Came Before Two of This Author's Falls

To get the ball rolling, I will share two prideful falls of my own, one figurative and one literal.

In my early thirties, a special program opened up in my small city for local state employees to pursue a doctorate in clinical psychology while remaining employed full-time. Our local state university provided the classrooms for psychologists from a professional school in Chicago to come down and teach us on weekends. The university supplied some of its own professors, too, and local clinics and hospitals provided us with ample opportunities for clinical practice.

Anyway, I took advantage of the program, and by the time I graduated, I was itching to work as a full-fledged psychologist. I grabbed the very first job that opened up in an area of psychology I had not been formally trained in, even though it required my wife to leave her job of two decades, and for us to sell our beloved first house and relocate, along with our two young children, to another city. I had never really failed at any major academic or work task I had undertaken, and the possibility of failure or a mismatch with my talents had never even crossed my prideful mind.

Fast-forward not even six months later. On the day that I opened a letter from the state of Indiana showing I had achieved the highest psychology licensing score in the state and, indeed, had set my own school's all-time record, I was in the midst of my first (and, thank God, only) depressive episode and trying to figure out how to return to my old job, which would require a voluntary demotion.

At this time, I was in the midst of my years of atheism. I did not believe in God (though I would find that he believed in me). Still, through his grace and with the help of family and good friends, I was indeed able to get my old job back and move through the ranks in a few years to a higher position than the one I had left. I was able to regain my part-time teaching position at the local university, my wife got her old job back, and our children returned to the schools and the friends that they loved.

To put the icing on the cake, while we were unable to get back the first house my wife and I bought together, through the grace of God (and a wonderful Baptist minister and his family who were relocating back to their home state), we were able to return to the house that had once been my parents', the house that I grew up in and that was out of the family for over fifteen years! Within two years of being literally home, the Holy Spirit led me to the writings of St. Thomas Aquinas, and I found myself back home in the Catholic Church, too. God is so good, even to the prideful, if we but humbly have faith in him and ask for his forgiveness.

Finally, on a more literal but less serious note, be aware that not only can swollen, overconfident pride lead us to a fall, but its silly sidekick vainglory can too. One fine summer day a decade or so ago, while out jogging in shorts, I looked down (not a good idea) to admire the fact that my usually ivory white legs had actually acquired some suntan. The instant I started to relish this simple moment of vainglory, I fell to the sidewalk and scraped up both tanned knees and both palms. While I hoped at the time that no one was looking, I learned that vainglory was not my friend. It too leads to a fall—and makes for a horrible running partner!

- OK then, are there times in *your* life when pride or vainglory went before your fall?

- What did you do to get back up?

- What lessons of humility did you learn?

- Have you thought about them lately and put them into practice?

Humility Lived Saint Story #4

St. Catherine of Siena (1347–1380)

I say that this tree has seven branches drooping to the earth, on which grow the flowers and leaves in the way I have told you. These branches are the seven mortal sins which are full of many and diverse wickednesses, contained in the roots and trunk of self-love and of pride, which first made both branches and flowers of many thoughts, the leaves of words, and the fruits of wicked deeds. They stand drooping to the earth because the branches of mortal sin can turn no other way than to the earth.[135]

–St. Catherine of Siena

One's origins don't get much lowlier than St. Catherine of Siena's. We saw in chapter 2 that she was one of twenty-five children of a father who was a cloth dyer. Further, Catherine remained illiterate until the age of thirty, when her humility and love of Christ were rewarded with a miracle.

Her spiritual mentor and biographer, Blessed Raymond of Capua, reports that she wanted to read so she could pray the Divine Praises and Canonical Hours, but the efforts of a friend to teach her the alphabet didn't get far after several weeks. Then Catherine prayed that Jesus himself would be her instructor. But she only wanted this if it was Christ's will, being willing to remain unable to read the Psalms or anything else if Our Lord did not will it.

After this prayer, Catherine began reading with no trouble. In fact, Raymond noted, as indicating a miracle, that she read too quickly to distinguish the syllables of the words. Christ also miraculously enabled her to write. She went on to write her first letter in 1377 after seeing a vision of Jesus with St. Thomas Aquinas. Catherine's famous letters and *Dialogue* rival the writings of the poet Dante in their masterful use of Italian.

Catherine's *Dialogue* is suffused with magnificently expressed spiritual lessons dictated by God during states of mystical ecstasy. My, what letters she wrote! This poor, humble, uneducated lay Dominican wrote letters to cardinals, popes, and public officials, always seeking peace by encouraging recipients to do the will of God. Her greatest and best-known triumph, as we briefly mentioned before, was to persuade the pope to bring the seat of the papacy back to Rome. The absence of the papacy derived from conflicts between the papacy and the French crown. When Clement V, a Frenchman, was elected pope in 1305, he declined to move to Rome and, in 1309, set up court in the city of Avignon, France. He and the next six popes stayed in Avignon for the next sixty-eight years, until the personal face-to-face admonitions of Catherine of Siena convinced Pope Gregory XI to come back home to Rome.

Of special relevance to our fourth chapter, as we saw in this essay's opening quotation, Catherine wrote movingly and metaphorically about the seven deadly sins as decaying, dying branches of a person's tree of life. She goes on to say that these sins are so deadly to life because the things of the earth that they droop toward can never fulfill them: "They are insatiable and unbearable to themselves," always "unquiet, longing and desiring ... something finite."[136] Our tree can only be made straight when we truly understand and accept our natures as described by the words of God to St. Catherine: "Man is placed above all creatures, and not beneath them, and he cannot be satisfied or content except in something greater than himself. Greater than himself there is nothing but Myself, the Eternal God."[137]

St. Catherine, pray for us, that we might conquer sin by embracing the humility that finds rest only in God.[138]

PART III

Humility Ascends

Christ's Passion is the cause of our ascending to heaven, properly speaking, by removing the hindrance which is sin, and also by way of merit: whereas Christ's Ascension is the direct cause of our ascension, as by beginning it in Him who is our Head, with whom the members must be united.[139]

—St. Thomas Aquinas

In Parts I and II, we took a thorough look at all the parts and the tools we will need to build a temple of humility and virtue within our own souls. We have seen some ways in which humility undergirds all virtues and helps defeat all sins. Now, it is time to take a look at some step-by-step instructions on how to build humility. In the first two chapters of Part III, following St. Thomas' lead in his analysis of humility, we will begin by looking at the ideas of two of the Church's great theological doctors who described a series of "steps" or "degrees" by which we can ascend to higher levels of humility—the good Lord willing, all the way to heaven. In our last chapter, we will look at a picture of complete and perfected humility, as we examine the life and lessons of Jesus Christ with special attention on his explicit call that we become gentle and humble like him.

Let's begin at the first rung of a great Benedictine's ladder.

Chapter 5

HUMILITY CLIMBS
A TWELVE-STEP LADDER

Holy Scripture, brethren, cries out to us, saying,
"Everyone who exalts himself shall be humbled, and he
who humbles himself shall be exalted."[140]

—St. Benedict of Nursia (c. 480–547)

St. Thomas Aquinas' personal humility rings out loudly in every page of his *Summa Theologica* in how he clearly listens to, respects, and accurately presents arguments contrary to his own in the series of "objections" that begin every one of his articles. Never pretending to achieve his great insights on his own and, indeed, almost never mentioning himself at all, Thomas cites dozens of Church Fathers and Doctors *many thousands* of times in the *Summa.*

A Dominican Helps Us Climb the Benedictine Ladder of Humility

One special treat in the *Summa* (II-II.161.6) is our great Dominican's commentary on the "twelve steps of humility" of the Father of the Benedictines (and Father of Monasticism) found within chapter 7 of the seventy-three chapters of St. Benedict's famous *Rule* for his order.

They are presented here in the wording Thomas uses to summarize them in the *Summa*, but their order follows that of St. Benedict's *Rule*. In the first "objection" section, Thomas presents and addresses these steps in the opposite order of Benedict's presentation to make some important theological points. We will address them very soon. For now, I will point out that we need not be medieval monks or friars to profit from the timeless wisdom of these two great saints regarding the steps of humility. So, let's start our trip up the ladder.

St. Benedict's Twelve Degrees of Humility[141]

1.	"To fear God and to be always mindful of everything that God has commanded."
2.	"Not to delight in fulfilling one's own desires."
3.	"To subject oneself to a superior."
4.	"To embrace patience by obeying under difficult and contrary circumstances."
5.	"To confess one's sin."
6.	"To think oneself worthless and unprofitable for all purposes."
7.	"To believe and acknowledge oneself viler than all."
8.	"To do nothing but to what one is exhorted by the common rule of the monastery."
9.	"To maintain silence until one is asked."
10.	"Not to be easily moved, and disposed to laughter."
11.	"Not to be loud of voice."
12.	"To be 'humble not only in heart, but also to show it in one's very person, one's eyes fixed on the ground.'"

Thomas starts by presenting a total of five objections that claim, for various reasons, that St. Benedict made some missteps in laying out his twelve-step program of humility. The first, most lengthy objection summarizes all twelve steps and then offers two criticisms:

- First, that these steps are supposed to be about humility, but some steps pertain to other virtues like obedience and patience. (Hopefully, readers of Part I would object to this objection, since humility pertains to and supports *all* the virtues!)

- Second, some of the steps seem to support *false* conceptions, which is never consistent with virtue, "namely to declare oneself more despicable than all men, and to confess and believe oneself to be in all ways worthless and unprofitable. Therefore these are unfittingly placed among the degrees of humility." (Perhaps you think that this objection is a little harder to refute. We will find out what Thomas had to say.)

The Angelic Doctor Ascends and Descends Benedict's Ladder

Whenever I think of "spiritual ladders"—such as the way the seven gifts of the Holy Spirit ascend like a ladder from fear of the Lord up to wisdom, as we saw in chapter 1—I think back to Jacob's ladder: "And he dreamed that there was a ladder set up on the earth, and the top of it reached to heaven; and behold, the angels of God were ascending and descending on it!" (Genesis 28:12). Well, Thomas is known as the Angelic Doctor, and in explaining how we ascend St. Benedict's ladder, he first presents them in descending order. Let's see why.

Thomas believes Benedict's twelve steps are laid out most fittingly indeed, as he demonstrates with intriguing and nuanced arguments. He begins by reiterating that humility essentially has to do with our *appetites* or *willful desires*. It "restrains the impetuosity" of our souls, to keep us from desiring inordinate great things (like the presumption that desires heaven without full submission to God's law and grace, or vainglorious desires for honors we do not deserve); "yet its rule is in the cognitive faculty, in that we should not deem ourselves to be above what we are." (Recall that we began our own discussion of humility with how it perfects the cognitive, intellectual virtues in their search for truth.) Further, "the principle and origin of both these things is the reverence we bear to God."

Thomas goes on to explain that humility's "inward disposition" brings us to show "outward signs in words, deeds, and gestures, which manifest that which is hidden within." This is the case for all virtues, St. Thomas says, citing Sirach 19:29: "a man is known by his appearance, and a sensible man is known by his face, when you meet him." The twelve degrees address both inward and outward elements, and they also address "*the root of humility*," St. Benedict's first step "*that a man fear God and bear all His commandments in mind.*"

Thomas notes that three of the steps or degrees have to do specifically with our *appetites*, so we don't inappropriately take our own excellence as our goal. This is done first "by not following one's own will," which we see in the second step "*not to delight in fulfilling one's own desires.*" The third step, "*to subject oneself to a superior*," regulates one's will by subjecting it to a superior's discernment, and the fourth step, "*to embrace patience by obeying under difficult and contrary circumstances*," keeps one from being turned aside from obeying the superior's will even when obstacles arise.

The next three steps regard the *cognitive* aspect of humility by acknowledging the true extent of our own weaknesses or limitations. "*To confess one's sin*," the fifth step, clearly owns up to one's own failings. In addition, "*to think oneself worthless and unprofitable for all purposes*," the sixth step, judges oneself unable to achieve "great things" on one's own power, and "*to believe and acknowledge oneself viler than all*," the seventh step, involves the decision to "put others before oneself."

All the steps above referring to the *inward* signs of humility, Thomas then details the steps that focus on its *outward* manifestations. The eighth step, "*to do nothing but to what one is exhorted by the common rule of the monastery*," regards the deeds involved in work, which should not be done out of the "ordinary way" to make tasks easier on oneself or to draw attention to oneself. Two other steps involve the use of words, "*to maintain silence until one is asked*," the ninth step, and "*not to be loud of voice*," the eleventh. The other steps, he says, deal with "outward gestures." "*To be 'humble not only in heart, but also to show it in one's very person, one's eyes fixed on the ground,'"* the twelfth, checks "haughty looks," and *"not to be easily moved, and disposed to laughter,"* the tenth, reins in "laughter and other signs of senseless mirth."

Why Did Thomas Place the Ladder Upside Down?

In response to the first argument of the first objection, that Benedict's degrees pertain to other virtues like patience and obedience rather than humility, Thomas replies, "There is nothing unbecoming in ascribing to humility those things that pertain to other virtues, since, just as one vice arises from another, so, by a natural sequence, the act of one virtue proceeds from the act of another." (Whew! Our first three chapters can remain in this book!)

In replying to the objection that it is *false* to declare oneself the most despicable or worthless of all men, Thomas brings St. Augustine and St. Paul to St. Benedict's defense. We can state *truly* that we are "the most despicable" people "as regards the hidden faults which we acknowledge in ourselves, and the hidden gifts of God which others have." This is a truly wonderful insight borrowed from Augustine, who wrote, *"Bethink you that some persons are in some hidden way better than you, although outwardly you are better than they."*[142] Further, one can legitimately declare oneself incompetent "and useless in respect of one's own capability, so as to refer all one's sufficiency to God," as Paul writes: "Not that we are sufficient of ourselves to claim anything as coming from us; our sufficiency is from God" (2 Corinthians 3:5).

Finally, let's look at the upside-down ladder. Thomas says that a person "arrives at humility in two ways."

The first and main way, reflected in St. Benedict's original order (starting with fear of God and ending with keeping one's eyes to the ground), is through the gift of *God's grace*, "and in this way the inner man precedes the outward man."

Secondly, our *human effort* helps us grow in humility as we work to rein in "the outward man," in terms of our behaviors, like gestures, deeds, and words, "and afterwards succeed ... in plucking out the inward root." This way is shown if we look at the twelve degrees in their reverse order.

Thomas was well aware that the seven gifts of the Holy Spirit were described in Isaiah 11:2–3 in order of their descent from God to man, from wisdom down to fear of the Lord. Setting them up in their reverse order, from fear of the Lord to wisdom—from least to greatest—forms a spiritual ladder we can climb! Perhaps this visual image will make things a little clearer:

THE "CHIEF WAY" TO GROW IN HUMILITY	THE "SECOND WAY" TO GROW IN HUMILITY
Benedict's original order Outer person last	**Thomas' presentation** Inner person last
12. Show humility in heart and eyes	12. Fear and obey God
11. Don't speak loudly	11. Relinquish desires
10. Avoid excess laughter	10. Submit to a superior
9. Be silent unless asked	9. Embrace patience
8. Obey the common rules	8. Confess your sins
7. Think yourself worse than others	7. Think yourself worthless
6. Think yourself worthless	6. Think yourself worse than others
5. Confess your sins	5. Obey the common rules
4. Embrace patience	4. Be silent unless asked
3. Submit to a superior	3. Avoid excess laughter
2. Relinquish personal desires	2. Don't speak loudly
1. Fear God and obey the Commandments	1. Show humility in heart and eyes
God's grace Inner person first	**Human effort** Outer person first

Both ways of approaching and looking at these steps make great psychological sense. Our thoughts, emotions, and behaviors are always intertwined and interrelated. In cognitive approaches to psychotherapy, an emphasis is placed on changing a person's thinking and general ways of looking at the world as a means to promote new, healthier behaviors. St. Benedict's original ordering of the steps of humility has this cognitive-to-behavioral, "inner person"-to-"outer person" approach, and yet it taps into an infinitely higher power than the human mind itself in the form of the graces God gives us (fear of the Lord, of course, being one of the gifts of the Holy Spirit).

Still, sometimes in therapy when a person has a hard time changing his or her thinking patterns, the therapist may recommend changing *behaviors* (the outward person) first. The simplest example I can think would be to force oneself to smile or laugh when you are feeling a little down. It is hard to maintain thoughts that contradict our outward behaviors.

So, with this little insight from our two great saints, we might strive to climb the ladder of humility through either a grace-based inward-to-outward path or an effort-based outward-to-inward path on any given day. Of course, as Thomas was so fond of saying, grace perfects nature.[143] God made both human effort and supernatural grace to work together hand in hand, from the small human hand of effort to the vast divine hand of God's grace. (Want a visual reminder of this idea? I suggest you refer to the Sistine Chapel's ceiling, where Michelangelo has unforgettably pictured the outstretched hands of man and God in the painting of the creation of Adam.)

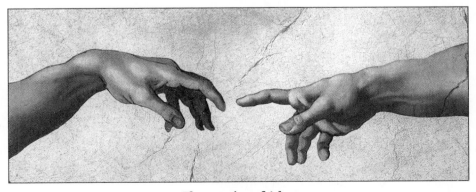

The creation of Adam

St. Thomas' Analysis
of St. Benedict's Twelve Degrees of Humility

Root of Humility	Inward Dispositions (appetitive or cognitive)	Outward Signs (deeds, words, gestures)
1. To fear God and keep his commandments	2. Not to delight in fulfilling one's desires (appetitive)	8. To do nothing outside of the rule (deeds)
	3. Subjection to one's superior (appetitive)	9. To maintain silence (words)
	4. To maintain patience under hardships (appetitive)	10. Not to be easily moved to laughter (gestures)
	5. To acknowledge and confess sins (cognitive)	11. Not to speak loudly (words)
	6. To think oneself worthless (cognitive)	12. To keep one's eyes fixed on the ground (gestures)
	7. To think oneself worse than others (cognitive)	

So then, we may well climb the ladder of humility from inside out, so to speak, from outside in, or by some combination of the two. However we climb them, the twelve steps of humility provide a lot of Benedictine and Dominican wisdom to ponder. Let's summarize some of St. Thomas' insights.

Climbing Benedict's Ladder for the Lay Person Today

I hope and pray there are Benedictine and Dominican readers of these pages, but even if so, you are certainly not of Benedict's sixth century or Thomas's thirteenth century. I imagine most readers are twenty-first-century lay people like me and are wondering how 1500-year-old rules for monks can help us acquire humility today. Rest assured that St. Benedict has provided *timeless*, *human* lessons for all of us in any century. Let's consider a few lessons for each rung of his ladder.

Nourishing the Root of Humility

1. We have seen that **fear of the Lord** is the beginning not only of wisdom but of humility. Thomas notes that fear of the Lord starts in our souls in its lowest form as a *servile fear* of incurring God's punishment. As we grow in our love of the Lord, as "perfect love casts out fear" (1 John 4:18) our servile fear is transformed within our hearts to the loving *filial fear* that fears not only our own punishment but fears offending or letting down God, who loves us so much. We show him our love by **following his commandments** (see John 14:15), including Christ's call to become "gentle and lowly in heart" (Matthew 11:29) like him. Clearly then, Benedict's first step toward humility is taken by putting God first in our hearts through a holy fear, reverence, and love of the Lord.

Transforming Our Inward Selves: The Will

2. When we **rein in our desires to fulfill our own wishes**, we follow the simple algebraic formula of St. Maximilian Kolbe (1894–1941), namely: $V + v = S$, where capital V stands for God's will, (*voluntas* being Latin for "will"); small v stands for our will, and S stands for sanctity. An even simpler formula is $V = v$. (Come to think of it, let's make it easier still by translating it into English as $W = w$.) We should

strive to make our own wills match the will of God. If we have the humility to regulate our own desires so they match and unite with the will of God, we will achieve holiness on earth and bliss in heaven.

St. Kolbe practiced the mathematics he preached to such a degree that in the midst of World War II, he volunteered to take the place of a stranger, a man with a wife and children, to die a slow death of starvation in Auschwitz, the horrific Nazi concentration camp. (This act so moved our second son, he took Maximilian's name at his Confirmation.) God willing, we will never face such a test in uniting our own wills with God's, but can St. Kolbe's example help give us the strength to become more submissive to God's will in the far less trying trials of our own lives?

A simple way to practice this slaying of our own willful desires is by seeing Christ in our neighbor and by following our neighbor's will in routine matters. (Now, does your family always have to go to the restaurant *you* choose, watch the movies *you* want to watch, go on vacation where *you* want to go, etc.?)

3. Lay people do not take a vow of **obedience** to formally subject themselves to the will of a religious superior, but there are many roles in life in which we relate to those in places of higher honor or authority than our own, be it as children to parents, employees to bosses, or the like. Though we must ultimately follow our own formed consciences in deciding what to do in ethically questionable matters, can we train ourselves, under normal circumstances, to follow our leaders *without grumbling or resentment*?

In fact, get a load of this from good St. Benedict himself: "Above all, let not the evil of murmuring appear for any reason whatsoever in the least word or sign. If anyone is caught at it, let him be placed under very severe discipline."[144] How interesting that while in the fortieth chapter of his rule Benedict permitted his monks up to one *hemina* (about one cupful) of wine per day, in his thirty-fourth chapter he permits no *whining* whatever!

And here is another thing to consider, that builds upon our last lesson. Even regarding equals, like a spouse or coworkers of the same rank, we need to ask ourselves to what extent we are willing to take their lead at times and not always demand to do things our way.

4. We discussed **maintaining patience under hardships** when we looked at the virtue of patience in chapter 2. Can you think of a particular person who frequently tries your patience? If so, can you pray for God's help in relating to him or to her the very next time you meet, without lashing out or getting upset? Perhaps you will recall that this person's behavior, despite how grating it may be, somehow makes sense to him from his own perspective? St. Benedict bids us to remember that Christ told us to "bless those who curse you, pray for those who abuse you" (Luke 6:28).

If we get really good at this, we might even come to enjoy the kind of tallying St. James recommends: "Count it all joy, my brethren, when you meet various trials, for you know that the testing of your faith produces steadfastness" (James 1:2).

Transforming Our Inward Selves: The Mind

5. Benedict states in his fifth step of humility that the monk is to "hide from his Abbot none of the evil thoughts that enter his heart or the sins committed in secret," and instead he should "humbly confess them." Though probably few readers are monks, as for **acknowledging and confessing sins,** we can strive to acquire the habit of facing up to the facts of reality by admitting to our loved ones, friends, or coworkers when we have been mistaken or acted badly. Further, like monks, we can and should avail ourselves of the sacrament of Reconciliation to confess mortal sins, and even venial sins, to God through his priest, to receive absolution, and restore the flow of supernatural grace into our souls.

6. **"To think oneself worthless."** For people who do not grasp the gist of Christian humility, this is precisely the kind of thing that gets their knickers in a twist, as the British are wont to say. Remember David and his worms (Psalm 22:6)? Or think of Job and his maggots (Job 25:6). Well here's another verse St. Benedict cites when expounding on this step: "I was stupid and ignorant, I was like a beast toward you" (Psalm 73:22). David said this was the way he was when his "soul was

embittered" and he "was pricked in heart" (Psalm 73:21), before he turned to the Lord. We must remember, too, this means that through humility we cannot accomplish any lofty thing purely *on our own power*, but *assisted by God's grace* the sky is the limit. (Actually, heaven is.) King David himself tells us as much in the following verses: "Nevertheless I am continually with you; you hold my right hand. You guide me with your counsel, and afterward you will receive me to glory" (Psalm 73: 23–24).

7. **"To think oneself worse than others."** Now that's another knicker-twister for some! We should all recall here the wonderful insight of St. Augustine. Humility, like an honest court of law, seeks the truth about ourselves, the whole truth, and nothing but the truth. We can so easily tend to remember our own good deeds and accomplishments while forgetting how often we fall so woefully short, while we can apply just the opposite bias toward others. What a powerful thing to ponder not only our hidden weaknesses but the hidden gifts of God to others.

In this regard I can mention a piece of humble pie that I have eaten. During my twenty-five years of atheism, I considered myself a better truth-seeker than most since I believed I was following reason wherever it led me. Indeed, I even wished that I could believe in God, but I could not honestly do so. Well, when I finally came to read St. Thomas Aquinas, my stubborn reason had no choice but to submit to the truth of his arguments and once again take a great leap of faith. Though it seemed in some ways like I brought myself back to the Faith by my own bootstraps (or bookcases) little did I know that several family members and friends had been praying for years I would return to the Faith. I can now thank God for their humbly "hidden gifts" of prayer (hidden to me at the time, anyway) that helped bring me back to where I belong!

One more lesson from many decades past also comes to mind. Please join me in the third-grade classroom of St. Agnes School. It is the spring of 1969. Sister has to pay a quick visit to the second-grade teacher whose classroom is right across the library from ours. She asks us to be quiet and behave while she's gone for just a few minutes. The boys and girls sit bolt upright with perfect posture, hands crossed upon their desks, and facial expressions befitting the highest choirs of angels.

One boy (with straight As in conduct, no less) is sitting near the front and observes that the minute the second-grade classroom door closes behind Sister, pandemonium breaks out in third grade, with raucous giggling and banter. Soon that door is seen to open, and the third-grade classroom is transformed in an instant once more into seraphic silence.

Now, when Sister walks back in, that one little boy, morally reviled by the infamy of his peers, who were clearly much viler than he, calls Sister over and tells her exactly what happened. Whereupon Sister instantly and simply replies, "Kevin, don't be a tattletale!" I ran into Sister just a few years ago, and she did not remember the incident, but I have never forgotten the lesson.

Indeed, in my office, we had an anonymous suggestion box, and its messages were read aloud by administrators during large staff meetings. Occasionally, a note would name names for all kinds of discretions, like perhaps someone's lunch hour that the note-writer had observed stretching into sixty-eight and one-half minutes. When I would tell my wife about such incidents when I got home, she would say, "The person who wrote that note obviously did not have Sister in the third grade!"

If we keep in mind that in some ways we may be viler than those we accuse of various villainies, the log in our eye outweighing their speck, we will climb one rung higher on the ladder of humility.

Humility in Outward Words, Signs, and Deeds

8. **To do nothing outside the rule of the monastery**. Thomas said this degree of humility addresses our work, and perhaps the most famous motto that sums up the Benedictine life is *ora et labora*—"pray and work." True, we can't work according to the rules of the monastery if we do not live in a monastery. Still, that doesn't mean we can scratch this degree of humility off our to-do lists.

   Even if we have retired from a formal job, we all still have some kind of work to get done in our daily lives, and we must remember that "in all toil there is profit" (Proverbs 14:23). The work involved in any honest occupation or avocation is worthwhile on its own account, but Thomas notes that Benedict's rule means that work "should not depart from the ordinary way." Perhaps he means we should do the work we are assigned in the proper manner, to the best of our ability, and for the right reason—to accomplish the good the work itself provides and to glorify God thereby, rather than to try to draw attention to our own excellence at getting the job done! The next time we are faced with any task, can we keep our noses to the grindstone without looking around to see if anyone notices how hard we are grinding?

9. As for **maintaining silence**, while few of us live in a monastery with a rule of silence,[145] we could all foster growth in humility by being mindful of situations in which we talk too much. How can we treat others as better than ourselves (or even as good) if we dominate conversations and hardly let our family members, friends, coworkers, or others get a word in edgewise?

    A good rule of thumb when engaged in conversation is to try to allot yourself no greater a percentage of time speaking than any others in the conversation. So, if you are talking to one person, try not to talk more than half of the time. In a letter St. Thomas wrote in response to a young friar who had asked his advice about how to study and learn, two of Thomas' dozen or so simple bits of advice were to "be slow to speak" and "above all, flee from aimless conversations."[146] If you do these things, you will display respect for your conversation partner, improve your listening skills, grow more docile—and be much less likely to talk yourself hoarse!

10. As for **not being easily moved to laughter**, St. Benedict reminds us that "a fool raises his voice when he laughs, but a clever man smiles quietly" (Sirach 21:20). After all, there is a lot of serious prayer and work to be done in a monastery. I suppose that especially for young novices, it might take some serious training to keep oneself from bursting out laughing if the abbot were to slip on a banana peel or something of that sort. A more measured and less disruptive response might be to keep one's eyes toward the ground (see step twelve) and

simply smile to oneself (as per Sirach)—unless, perhaps, the abbot himself burst out laughing first!

Indeed, there is a delightful little tale along these lines involving the man who followed St. Dominic as the master general of the Order of Preachers (the Dominicans). Recall that St. Albert the Great was very influential in the life of St. Thomas Aquinas as a Dominican. Well, this man, Blessed Jordan of Saxony, was the man who recruited St. Albert (along with countless other young men).

As the story goes, one night in 1229, a group of young new Dominicans got the giggles and broke out laughing during Compline (nighttime prayer). A more experienced brother rebuked them, letting them know that they must be quiet. Perhaps if you have been in a similar situation you will understand how their laughter grew even louder despite their attempts to stifle it. When Compline was over, Blessed Jordan told them, "Laugh to your heart's content," adding that they could be as merry as they pleased, as new Dominicans, "after breaking from the devil's thraldom."[147]

It might not surprise you to learn that St. Thomas writes about laughter (since he writes about almost everything else), stating it is unreasonable "to be burdensome to others, by offering no pleasure to others, and by hindering their enjoyment." Further, he points out, "A man who is without mirth, not only is lacking in playful speech, but is also burdensome to others, since he is deaf to the moderate mirth of others."[148]

Now, St. Benedict writes that one should not be "easily moved" to laughter, or, in some translations, moved to "undue laughter or frivolity." His rule did *not* rule out the joys of humor and laugher all together. Moderate mirth is a good thing, but to be moderate, mirth should be expressed in appropriate ways, in appropriate situations, at appropriate times, and never through vulgarity or mockery of others. If we are to train ourselves to become more humble, we should moderate our mirth and steer clear of both the extremes of sourpuss humorlessness and of silly buffoonery. Further, to grow in humility we should train ourselves to laugh not *at* but *with* others when it truly is a laughing matter.

11. As for developing the habit of **not speaking loudly**, an unduly loud voice can display one's undue sense of self-importance or intention to dominate others. St. Benedict says we should speak quietly, humbly, and without an excess of wordiness. And indeed, if we speak a little less loudly we may not only model humility but help our conversation partners build up *their* listening skills!

12. To **keep one's eyes to the ground** is certainly an interesting recommendation, with many possible implications. To begin, note how the haughty are sometimes described as walking around with their noses in the air. This step is certainly a quick fix for that, but I think St. Benedict had much more in mind. Indeed, he explained this step in some detail, advising that

> a monk not only have humility in his heart but also by his very appearance make it always manifest to those who see him. That is to say that whether he is at the Work of God, in the oratory, in the monastery, in the garden, on the road, in the fields or anywhere else, and whether sitting, walking or standing, he should always have his head bowed and his eyes toward the ground.[149]

St. Thomas wrote about a vice that Catholic theologians had dubbed *curiositas* (related to the Latin word *cura* for "care"), which is an unbridled curiosity that cares too often or too much about things that are sinful or simply not important. When our eyes are flitting all over the place looking for sundry diversions and amusements, we are not in a good position to focus on and ponder things that are truly important.

Still, there is a virtue that directly counters *curiositas*, and it is called *studiositas* or studiousness. A great ally to the intellectual virtues of knowledge, understanding, and wisdom, studiousness helps us focus our eyes, and our minds, on the things that matter the most. To a monk, this would include things like prayer and work, and come to think of it, those should be among the things important to us as well.

Of course, this advice is also a literal instance of the age-old admonition to practice "custody of the eyes" by training ourselves not to look at titillating temptations toward sin.

What Rests at the Top of St. Benedict's Ladder?

What should happen if a monk (or if you or I) were to successfully climb all twelve steps toward humility? St. Benedict himself has supplied the answer:

> Having climbed all these steps of humility, therefore, the monk will presently come to that perfect love of God which casts out fear. And all those precepts which formerly he had not observed without fear, he will now begin to keep by reason of that love, without any effort, as though naturally and by habit. No longer will his motive be the fear of hell, but rather the love of Christ, good habit and delight in the virtues which the Lord will deign to show forth by the Holy Spirit in His servant now cleansed from vice and sin.[150]

Now that sounds like a ladder worth ascending!

Humility's Holy Toolbox:
Equipment for Climbing St. Benedict's Ladder

1. **Prayer** – Do you wonder how St. Benedict would have advised his monks to pray? Do you think he would have emphasized humility even in prayer? Do you think his rules about avoiding excess wordiness would be applied even when we pray to God? Well, let's see how you did. Here is St. Benedict's brief instruction "On Reverence in Prayer," chapter 20 in his *Rule*:

    > When we wish to suggest our wants to men of high station, we do not presume to do so except with humility and reverence. How much the more, then, are complete humility and pure devotion necessary in supplication of the Lord who is God of the universe! And let us be assured that it is not in saying a great deal that we shall be heard, but in purity of heart and in tears of compunction. Our prayer, therefore, ought to be short and pure, unless it happens to be prolonged by an inspiration of divine grace.[151]

2. **Honor the sacrament of Matrimony.** We are looking for special connections between each of the sacraments and growth in humility. Now, neither Benedict nor his holy sister, St. Scholastica, were married, and neither were their monks or nuns, but all of them, like all of us, knew that they must humbly pursue the particular vocation God laid upon their hearts.

Traditionally, the sacrament of Matrimony was linked with the virtue of temperance, since temperance guides our sexual desires toward healthy, holy expression. Recall, if you will, that St. Thomas wrote his articles on humility in his discussion of temperance and all its allied virtues. Through temperance, we rein in worldly desires so that our eyes and hearts might focus most clearly on the things of God.

Again, I assume only a small number of you reading these pages are members of religious orders, but perhaps a large number of readers have experienced the sacrament of Matrimony yourselves, or at least grew up in a household sanctified by this sacrament.

If you are a husband and father or a wife and mother, consider the parallels between a Catholic monastery and a Catholic household (known as the "domestic church"). Have you considered how your role parallels that of an abbot or abbess? What kind of a "rule" have you set up in your household for the bodies and souls under your charge? Does it include any kinds of recommended steps for growing in humility through fostering a humble heart, humble thoughts, humble gestures and actions? If not, might you consider setting up some sort of such rule? If so, don't forget to follow your own rules (though your spouse and your children may well remind you if you don't).

Chapter 5 Summary and Reflections

We have climbed up and down St. Benedict's twelve-step ladder of humility, inspected it, and found it sturdy and reliable to this day as an aid to help us rise toward heaven. I will leave you with just a couple of parting thoughts.

- Are there any of the twelve steps that you especially need to work on climbing? If so, are they steps that involve accepting *God's grace* to grow in humility, steps that involve training your *inward person* in will or in mind, or steps that involve training yourself in the *outward actions* of your words, deeds, and gestures? Can you think of things you can do to firm up your shakiest steps, to lighten the load of your ego, and make sure you don't fall?

- If you are ever prone to think like the infamous Pharisee and thank God you are not like other sinful people (see Luke 18:11), can you set aside a few minutes each day for the next few days to pray the tax collector's prayer—"God, be merciful to me a sinner" (Luke 18:13)—to call to mind your own "hidden faults," and to meditate on the possible "hidden gifts" of the others you live with, work with, or chance upon during the course of your day?

Humility Lived Saint Story #5:

St. Humilitas (1226–1310)

I go to the Lord, and he orders me to do this work, and then the Spirit of Jesus teaches me. And then and always the King of Creation is with me, who would not wish me to speak in ignorance, but I understand what I see, being fully instructed in what I think.[152]

—St. Humilitas

No sample of humble saints would be complete without the story of "St. Humility." (Don't worry if you have never heard of her, since I will humbly admit I hadn't either until I started writing this book!) Well, here is her humble story.

St. Humilitas was St. Thomas Aquinas' contemporary. Named Rosanesa at birth, she was born in 1226 and lived thirty-six years longer than the Angelic Doctor, who died in 1274. She also had something important in common with St. Benedict, since at age twenty-four she would go on to become a religious sister, alongside monks, in the double monastery of St. Perpetua. Prior to that she had been married, and after the death of two children after their baptisms, she and her husband both heeded God's call and became consecrated religious, he a monk, and she a nun, at the double monastery.

A biographer describes that Rosanesa "mortified herself by taking on the most humble and servile jobs. The other Sisters thought this was a passing phase but the superior of the two monasteries understood her virtue and renamed her Umiltà ("Humility").[153]

Though she was born to a high-ranking family, she, like St. Catherine of Siena, did not learn to read until she reached adulthood. When fellow sisters requested that she read from a book, "she obeyed humbly and from her mouth came words of the highest things"—but none of those things were in the book! Her first words were these: "Do not despise the work of God, which is always true and just, though it is hard. In heaven shall be raised what is always humble."

Later in life, St. Humilitas would begin building a monastery of her own in Florence, Italy, consecrated to St. John the Evangelist. Indeed, this lover of hard work began by finding the stones herself and placing them on a donkey! St. Humilitas is also known for a number of beautiful sermons she crafted. In the eighth sermon she wrote:

> While you, my teacher, are King, most sweet and kind, you speak to me, exhilarating me, and I speak, burning with desire through being loved by Christ. You teach me to speak and to know the truth. With me you are near and make me, your unworthy slave, speak and open my mouth with these words, which are not my own.

St. Humilitas, pray for us, that we might humble ourselves to hear God's voice, learn his lessons, and speak the truths the Holy Spirit whispers in our ears.[154]

Chapter 6

HUMILITY SCALES
A SEVEN-STORY MOUNTAIN

But humility is a great mountain, at whose summit there is full light, and a crowd of very good [honestarum] persons, that is the holy virtues. Its height is climbed by seven levels.[155]

—St. Anselm of Canterbury (c. 1033–1109)

St. Anselm of Canterbury, who wrote of a metaphorical mountain of humility, serves as a wonderful bridge between St. Benedict's ladder of humility and St. Thomas Aquinas' writings on both men's teachings. Before he became archbishop of Canterbury in Britain in 1093, Anselm, originally from Aosta, Italy, was a Benedictine monk and abbot. Due to his great philosophical and theological works, he has also been deemed the "Father of the Scholastics" and the "Scholastic Doctor," the first of the great systematic medieval theologians who often worked in school (university) settings, the greatest of whom was St. Thomas Aquinas!

Anselm had the greatest respect for the wisdom of his order's founder regarding the degrees of humility and, like Aquinas who would follow him, had a great penchant for analyzing and absorbing the teaching of great Church Fathers and Doctors to stimulate sublime insights of his own. Most interestingly, Anselm's seven-story mountain of humility appears in the context of Thomas' question on humility in the *Summa Theologica*: "Whether twelve degrees of humility are fittingly distinguished in the Rule of the Blessed Benedict?"[156]

A Ladder, a Bridge, and a Mountain of Humility

We saw in the previous chapter that Thomas found Benedict's twelve degrees most fitting, indeed. Here though, in the third objection in his article, Thomas summarizes an argument (not his own) that claims Benedict lists too many degrees because Anselm lists only seven!

So, if I might state this, just for fun, in the terms of the boxing ring:

> *Ladies and Gentlemen: Tonight we are going to see which great saint will be crowned the "Heavyweight World Champion Theologian of Humility." In this corner, hailing from Monte Cassino, Italy, "The Father of Monasticism," St. Benedict of Nursia! And in this corner, all the way from Canterbury, England, "The Father of Scholasticism," St. Anselm of Canterbury! Our special guest referee, known widely for his keen eye and unwavering fairness, is "The Angelic Doctor" himself, St. Thomas Aquinas!*

Before we move to ringside, let's briefly lay out St. Anselm's seven levels of humility in the wording used in Thomas' *Summa*.

St. Anselm's Seven Levels of Humility

1.	"To acknowledge oneself contemptible."
2.	"To grieve for this."
3.	"To confess it."
4.	"To convince others of this."
5.	"To bear patiently that this be said of us."
6.	"To suffer oneself to be treated with contempt."
7.	"To love being thus treated."

To Cut to the Chase (and Start Climbing the Mountain)

To cut to the chase of our imaginary heavyweight battle for the title of theological champion of humility, I imagine that St. Benedict and St. Anselm, as spiritual father and son, would rejoice in the chance to meet each other across the centuries, warmly embrace, refuse to engage in battle, and insist that the other be given the championship belt. (St. Thomas, without doubt, would memorize their every word and ask for signed copies of all their books.)

Now let's get down to some serious business. Thomas was able to draw a wealth of insights on humility from both Benedict's twelve-step ladder *and* Anselm's seven-story mountain. They in no way oppose each other. We saw some of the insights Thomas drew from Benedict in our last chapter, and now we move to his analysis of St. Anselm's scheme.

He begins by noting that all of Anselm's degrees can be boiled down to "knowledge, avowal, and desiring of one's own debasement." In other words, they can be reduced to humility's powers to lead us to *know ourselves* as we really are, to avow or *proclaim to others* this truth about ourselves, and to actively endure, seek out, and even *enjoy* the humiliating consequences. None of these are easy tasks, and they get tougher and tougher the further we climb up the mountain. Let's examine the seven levels one by one.

Climbing Our Own Mountains of Humility

St. Anselm addresses humility in several of his writings, especially in *De similitudinibus* (*On Likeness*) and the *Dicta Anselmi* (*Dictums of Anselm*).

Before describing the *mountain* of humility with beautiful, metaphorical imagery, not unlike the later writings of Dante, St. Anselm describes the *valley* of pride. When a person tries to set himself high through pride, he will fall far into pride's valley. "The thickness of its shadows," Anselm says, corresponds to the degree of "ignorance of self" the prideful show regarding how "contemptible" they are. Within those dark shadows the prideful are assaulted by all sorts of "evil beasts," which are the vices abusing all "who are ignorant of themselves" and their true nature.[157] Indeed, in the *Dicta Anselmi*, Anselm writes that a prideful person "will encounter cruelty like the lion, cunning like the fox, envy like the serpent, wrath like the toad, and the other vices like death-bringing living things in the same place." (Perhaps this will call to mind the seven deadly sins and their death-dealing daughters, all the spawn of pride, the "queen of the vices.")

The person who desires to disperse the shadows of self-ignorance and climb free of the valley of pride, must embrace humility, "which is the seat of truth." As he grows in self-knowledge and ascends the seven levels of the mountain of humility, he will find that its peak is bright with light, and he will be accompanied not by the beasts of vice, but by "a crowd of very good [*honestarum*] persons, that is the holy virtues." (We see that Anselm, too, acknowledges humility's foundational role in introducing us to all of the virtues.)

With good St. Anselm as our guide, let's get out our spikes and our ropes and begin our ascent to the summit of his seven-story mountain.

The Valley of Pride
and the Seven-Story Mountain of Humility

HUMILITY
Virtuous People
Self-Knowledge

7. To love being thus treated.

6. To suffer oneself to be treated with
    contempt.

5. To bear patiently that this be said of us.

4. To convince others of this.

3. To confess it.

2. To grieve for this.

1. To acknowledge oneself contemptible.

PRIDE
Beastly Vices and Sins
Self-Ignorance

1. **To acknowledge oneself contemptible.** Thomas sums this up tersely as acquiring "knowledge of one's own deficiency." Anselm elaborates, echoing Benedict (and Scripture) to say that we, like the apostle St. Paul, should consider others as better than ourselves (see Ephesians 3:8 and Philippians 2:3), by examining our consciences and calling to mind all the ways we have offended God's justice through our many sins. He concludes: "Who so judges himself, stands then at the first level of humility."

2. **To grieve for this.** Thomas says that "since it would be wrong for one to love one's own failings," this degree must follow the first. Anselm elaborates that if a person does not experience *dolor* ("pain or distress") for the transgressions he has committed, he truly lacks humility and does not deserve forgiveness. If I might reduce this step to the lingo of the weight room, St. Anselm tells us flat out: "No pain, no gain!" One cannot skip over this level of the mountain.

3. **To confess it.** Thomas says that this step involves "avowal of one's own deficiency." Anselm elaborates that the more "a person knows himself to be a sinner and is pained, the more he ought to confess it." Anselm states that many stall at this level of the mountain because while they realize their sinfulness and it causes distress, they conceal it out of shame "since it would make them blush to confess." He notes quite perceptively (and four hundred years before the Protestant Reformation that denied the sacrament of Reconciliation) that some people will decide to confess only to God himself and to do a heavier penance than would have been given by a confessor. "In this," Anselm warns, "they are entirely deceived." God already knows all their sins, since "everything is naked and open to Him. And so God wills that whosoever should sin against Him—as if God Himself did not know it—that person should confess it to another person in God's place, and by this sign it will be clearly proven that, even if God did not know of it, this person would truthfully open it and show it forth to Him." Further, "no matter how severe, doing penance without confession is always something lesser than making confession with a pure heart."

4. **To convince others of it.** Thomas notes that at this level, one goes further than declaring one's shortcoming and indeed seeks to "convince

another of it." Anselm elaborates that in sincerely confessing our failings we persuade our own will of our lowliness and need for humility. To be able to acknowledge our transgressions, to be distressed by them, and to judge ourselves is a worthy goal. But *a higher humility is attained when we allow ourselves to be judged by others*, when we expose our flaws for others to see but are not knocked back down the mountain by the boulders others may hurl at us from above.

5. **To bear patiently that this be said of us.** Arriving at Anselm's fifth level of the humility mountain, we recall the fourth rung of Benedict's ladder, "to embrace patience."

    Benedict extolled patience in *obeying and fulfilling difficult orders*, and Anselm extols patience in *bearing insults* from others, eloquently stating as follows: "This ought to be such a companion to each and every person that, whenever someone does any injury whatsoever, one receives it, as if the other person were to be doing one a great benefit." Thomas adds a wonderful insight from St. Gregory the Great: "There is nothing great in being humble towards those who treat us with regard, for even worldly people do this: but we should especially be humble towards those who make us suffer."[158]

    In essence, if we should arrive at level five, our response to insults or the exposure of our flaws will transform an indignant "How dare you!" to a patiently grateful "Thank you!" Let us pray to God for this excellent and rare level of humility.

6. **To suffer oneself to be treated with contempt.** Thomas notes that at this level, along with levels five and seven, the appetite "seeks, not outward excellence, but outward abasement, or bears it with equanimity, whether it consist of words or deeds." According to Anselm, "And we then, who have committed many things against our creator, we ought to humble ourselves just as zealously as we readily see ourselves to be in need of his indulgence." It is no easy thing, this willingness to seek out and suffer contempt from others. Our ultimate exemplar is certainly Jesus Christ himself, who willingly submitted to the most heinous abasement and contemptuous treatment *for our sake*, though he was *without sin*. We can pray for his guidance to scale

this high up the mountain to seek out and welcome the far smaller humiliations that others may make us suffer.

7. **To love being thus treated.** Thomas says that at the highest level we "even go so far as lovingly to embrace external abasement." Anselm says, "There is no doubt whether one will obtain indulgence, who not only judges himself worthy of punishment [on] account of his transgressions, but even desires to suffer retribution from all created beings as satisfaction to the creator."

Do you recall the *filial fear* that so loves God it dreads to offend him in any way? It also ardently desires to make right any wrongs our sins have done to God. To arrive at the peak of the mountain we must so accept, embrace, and reciprocate God's love that we long to make things right and honor him, regardless of how it shows we ourselves are unworthy of honor. Further, when we see that amends are being made to God, he will grant us a spiritual joy that overwhelms the pains of humiliation. "The greater you are, the more you must humble yourself; so you will find favor with God" (Sirach 3:18).

If any readers find it hard to imagine ever being able to "embrace external abasement," here is a simple thought to ponder. Thomas has explained that we love and desire whatever we truly believe is good for us. When we achieve what we love, we experience joy and peace. Now, sometimes we desire not only positive goods like virtues or pleasures, but what we could call negative goods, the cessation of things like vices or pains. If we could reach this final state of humility, we would put an end to all kinds of pains and difficulties that arise from a lack of humility, things like the stresses of keeping up a false, inflated images of ourselves—of maintaining false appearances.

Not "Bucket"—"Bouquet!"

To put this into simpler terms, some readers may be familiar with the British comedy show from the 1990s called *Keeping Up Appearances.* In every hilarious episode, the hapless heroine, Hyacinth Bucket (she falsely told everyone it was pronounced like "bouquet"), got herself and her family into all kinds of embarrassing, distressing situations because she kept trying to "keep up the appearance" that she and her family were wealthier, more accomplished, and of higher social status than they really were. In modern slang, she was constantly trying to make others think that she was "all that!" I particularly recall her horror at her friends discovering that her sister and her brother were poor, had simple tastes, and lived on the wrong side of town.

Anyway, if we could, through humility, become less worried about keeping up our own appearances, less worried about others seeing us as we truly are, "warts and all" as the saying goes, we would certainly attain more peace and tranquility—and might even come, with God's grace, to love it.

From Mount Olympus to the Mount of Olives

The greatest of the ancient philosophers recognized the value of the natural virtue of humility and taught some useful lessons on how to cultivate it. For example, the Stoic philosopher Epictetus says, "If someone reports back to you that so-and-so is saying bad things about you, do not reply to them but answer, 'Obviously he didn't know my other bad characteristics, since otherwise he wouldn't just have mentioned these.'"[159] The Stoics strove for an unruffled mental tranquility so that outside events, including personal insults, would not sway them from their pursuit of natural virtues.

While this is a noble goal, Christians aim even higher, since our ultimate goal is heaven, and our ultimate guide is Jesus Christ. When we ascend Christ's mountain of humility, we can learn not only to be unruffled when our flaws are pointed out but to welcome fraternal correction and to thank those who correct us and pray for them. The living saints who reach the mountain's seventh level have even come to love and enjoy the exposure of their flaws, since they know they must continue to learn the truth about themselves and to grow in humble holiness until their last day on earth. Hence they remain docile to their earthly teachers, even when the lessons are humiliatingly hard ones. Might we learn from them and strive to be in their number. What glorious perspectives we might attain from atop that seven-story mountain!

Humility's Holy Toolbox:

Mountain-Climbing Tools

1. **Prayer** – St. Anselm would have each one of us climb humility's mountain, yet he also knew ever so well that Christ commands us to love our neighbors as ourselves. Christ called us to climb humility's mountain (where he waits for us at the top), but he bids us to help our neighbors escape from the valley of pride and make the ascent along with us. Below is an excerpt of a prayer St. Anselm crafted to pray for his friends. Both love and humility ring out loud and clear. Shall we pray it together, in hopes that our friends will join us in some holy mountaineering?

> My good Lord, as your servant I long to
> pray to you for my friends,
> but as your debtor I am held back by my
> sins. For if I am not able to
> pray for my own pardon, how then can I
> dare to ask openly for your
> grace for others? I anxiously seek
> intercessors on my own behalf,
> how then shall I be so bold as to
> intercede for others? What shall I do,
> Lord God, what shall I do? You command
> me to pray for them and my
> love prompts me to do so, but my
> conscience cries out against me,
> saying that I should be concerned about
> my own sins, so that I tremble
> to speak for others. Shall I then leave off
> from doing what you command because

I have done what you have forbidden?
No, rather since I have presumed
so greatly in what is forbidden, all the
more will I embrace what is
commanded. So perhaps obedience may
heal presumption, and charity
may cover the multitude of my sins. So I
pray you, good and gracious
God, for those who love me for your sake
and whom I love in you.[160]

2. **The sacrament of Anointing of the Sick** – All sacraments confer grace, and we stand most receptive to grace when we stand in humility. The Anointing of the Sick has been paired with the virtue of hope. Hope, you will recall, looks forward to spending eternity in heaven with God and trusts that he will provide us in this life with all aids we need to get there.

   Anointing of the Sick indeed looks forward to the end of our life on earth and the beginning of our life in heaven, but it is not necessarily performed only near the end of life. Throughout history, it often was given at the point of death and was called Extreme Unction. When it is administered to the dying today, Anointing of the Sick, along with confession and the Viaticum (a word meaning supplies for the journey) of a final Communion are administered together in what is known as the last rites.

   So how might this sacrament help us grow in hope? Well, whether or not we have ever received it, simply knowing that this sacrament exists can bolster our hope of a life someday in heaven, since the sacrament itself is one of the aids God provides us if we need it to join him someday, forever.

   And how might this sacrament help us grow in *humility*? Well, of all the sacraments, this one reminds us most clearly of the simple, awesome fact that we are indeed "ashes to ashes, dust to dust." Every time we remember this fact it should motivate us to climb that mountain of humility so we can join God, the saints, and the angels at its top.

Chapter 6 Summary and Reflections

Together we climbed St. Anselm's seven-story mountain of humility. In our desire to escape the monstrous vices that fill the valley of pride and to rejoice with the noble virtues atop humility mountain, we saw the need to acknowledge what is contemptible in us, to feel sorry for our faults, to confess them aloud, to convince others of it, to bear patiently what is said about us, even to seek out correction and derision and come to love it.

Though he looked at humility with lenses of his own, we have seen how Anselm builds on the insight of his spiritual father, St. Benedict, to give us new insights into how humility grows through interior convictions and external actions. As we ponder how to incorporate Anselm's insights into our own ascents up the mountain of humility, we might ask ourselves questions like these:

- Have I examined my conscience lately for the monstrous vices within me spawned in the shadows of the valley of pride? Do I see how they deform the beauty and purity of my soul?

- Am I willing to acknowledge, admit, grieve over, and confess my faults, with a willingness to accept God's grace to renew my ascent up the mountain of humility?

- Are there any particular areas where I find it especially hard to relinquish my pride and willingly accept not only being "treated with contempt" but also helpful criticism and correction? If so, can I pray for God's aid and train myself in humility to climb out of pride's valley and climb higher up humility's mountain?

I will end by proclaiming to others (namely, you, dear reader) one such prideful, tender spot of my own. Being of a rather non-confrontational temperament by nature and an author of books by choice, I recall the wounds to my pride whenever negative reviews would come out on my first books. I felt distress, not because of my literary inadequacies but because others had pointed them out! Sometimes the criticisms were clearly unwarranted, as when atheists wrote negative reviews of one book without having read a word (which I knew because the review came online before the book was released!). Those were easy to bear and, in one case, I invited a reviewer to feel free to review the book again once he had had the chance to read it. Far more frequent, though, were reviews that pointed out real flaws. Now, while I cannot claim I have scaled high enough to love and enjoy such criticism, I can more patiently bear it and try to take the reviewers' advice to craft the next book just a little bit better.

Next, let's take a quick look at a saint who lived a life of joy and service at the peak of Mt. Humility.

Humility Lived Saint Story #6

St. Martin de Porres (1579–1639)

He excused the faults of others. He forgave the bitterest injuries, convinced that he deserved much severer punishments on account of his own sins. He tried with all his might to redeem the guilty; lovingly he comforted the sick; he provided food, clothing and medicine for the poor; he helped, as best he could, farm laborers and Negroes, as well as mulattoes, who were looked upon at that time as akin to slaves: thus he deserved to be called by the name the people gave him: "Martin of Charity." [161]

—St. John XXIII

St. Thomas Aquinas is often depicted holding in one hand a massive tome (his own *Summa Theologica*) and in the other hand a church (the Catholic Church), with a sun bursting forth in rays emblazoned across his chest (portraying the way he enlightens us). So what are we to make of a saint depicted with a broom, a dog, a cat, and a mouse? Perhaps this saint too can teach us firsthand lessons about humility lived.

Martin de Porres was born in Peru to Ana Velazquez, a woman of African heritage who had been a slave, and a highborn Spaniard named Juan de Porres, who was not married to his mother and, indeed, did not acknowledge Martin for some time. St. Martin, who grew up to care for the lowly and suffering and is the patron of mixed-raced people, is a marvelous saint of charity, as St. John XXIII made clear, and indeed of humility as well. In fact, though a barber, he was also highly sought after as a surgeon (the barbers of his day and time served as doctors, dentists, and pharmacists too.) He was also a man of great intelligence immersed in the writings of his fellow Dominican, St. Thomas Aquinas. Indeed, one story tells of two bright seminarians discussing what St. Thomas might say about a particular issue. Martin, overhearing while sweeping the floor, told them that Thomas had indeed addressed the issue and advised them just where to find the answer in the *Summa Theologica.*

Still, Martin never sought positions higher than those of barber, porter, bell ringer, and animal rescue clinic manager. He desired to join the Dominicans but did not even strive to become a religious brother at first, being quite content with the role of a lay brother of lowest rank. Records show he later became a Dominican brother but preferred to remain in the lay brother's garb.

St. Martin was so loved by the people around him that countless anecdotes have been told about his remarkable life. Alas, I have space to tell you just a few. There are a lot of stories involving Martin's love for animals (and their love for him), and many of these simple stories may convey much deeper messages.

For instance, it is told that in the early hours of the morning, when Martin needed to get up to ring the bell at his priory, a cat came to help him, tugging on his habit to wake him up. The color of the cat is representative of the work Martin did, for the cat was brown, black, and white. Martin, himself of mixed race, inspired the people of Peru, brown, black, and white, to unite in worship when they heard the priory's bell announcing Mass.

Another story demonstrates how St. Martin had scaled to the very top of St. Anselm's mountain, not only enjoying abasement from others but turning the situation around to his abuser's spiritual advantage.

As I have written elsewhere,

> In a time of great racial prejudice and discrimination, the dark-skinned, biracial Martin was often referred to as a mulatto dog, even at times by his brother friars ...

When people would taunt him by calling him a mulatto dog, Martin did not fight back, or merely shrug it off, but often sought these people out to do good works for them. When his friends would reprove him for this, he would say, 'These people truly know me.' In the most poignant example, he was nursing an older ailing priest scheduled to have his leg amputated the next day. The priest started berating him and called him a mulatto dog, perhaps envying Martin's youth, his joy, or his health. A witness said Martin chuckled to himself as he left the room. He discerned that the priest had been craving a salad seasoned with capers.[162] He came back the next day and served the priest such a salad. The priest savored his meal, begged Brother Martin's forgiveness, and indeed, his leg was healed. Would that we all could repay insults with such savory capers of kindness![163]

May Martin's humble example inspire us, whether we face grave injustices like he did or smaller opportunities to climb the mountain of humility.[164]

Chapter 7

HUMILITY RESTS UPON THE CROSS (AND IN THE TABERNACLE)

In the beginning was the Word, and the Word was with God, and the Word was God ... And the Word became flesh and dwelt among us, full of grace and truth.

—John 1:1, 14

Learn from me; for I am gentle and lowly in heart, and you will find rest for your souls. For my yoke is easy, and my burden is light.

—Matthew 11:29–30

God is of limitless power and magnitude. "Do I not fill heaven and earth? says the LORD" (Jeremiah 23:24). St. Thomas elaborates on God's infinite essence, presence, and power as follows:

> God is in all things by His *power*, inasmuch as all things are subject to His power; He is by His *presence* in all things, as all things are bare and open to His eyes; He is in all things by His *essence*, inasmuch as He is present to all as the cause of their being.[165]

When Infinite Immensity Chose to Become Small for Us

Now, if any being had no reason whatsoever to feel humble or lowly about anything, that being, of course, is Being Itself, the omnipotent, eternal "I AM" revealed to Moses (see Exodus 3:14), the source and font of creation. God later revealed himself as a Holy Trinity of Father, Son, and Holy Spirit, "one God in three persons, the 'consubstantial Trinity'" (CCC 253). We learned that all things were made through the Son, his Word (see John 1:3), and that through the power of the Holy Spirit, the almighty infinite Word chose to become small for the sake of our salvation, to take on human flesh and start life as we do, within the narrow confines of a mother's womb (see Luke 1:31).

Six centuries before his birth, a great prophet had foretold, "For the LORD has created a new thing on the earth: a woman protects a man" (Jeremiah 31:22). Thirteen centuries after his birth, St. Albert the Great declared the glorious "new" thing would be the union of divinity with humanity in this birth, since of course, the union of soul and body within man is nothing new at all. Some English translations use the word "compass" instead of "protects." St. Albert used the Latin translation of *circumdabit*, "enclose," noting the wondrous mystery that though Christ in his divinity is infinite and boundless, he would be enclosed within the confines of his earthly mother's womb.[166]

That act, the voluntary incarnation of the Word, the Son of God, retaining his divine nature while taking on a human nature as well, and all for our sake, was an act of humility and love that surpasses human understanding. As St. Paul stated so movingly, our Lord Jesus Christ "emptied himself, taking the form of a servant, being born in the likeness of men. And being found in human form he humbled himself and became obedient unto death, even death on a cross" (Philippians 2:7–8).

Why did he choose to do this? In the eloquent words of the *Catechism*:

> The Word became flesh to make us *"partakers of the divine nature"*: "For this is why the Word became man, and the Son of God became the Son of man: so that man, by entering into communion with the Word and thus receiving divine sonship, might become a son of God." "For the Son of God became man so that we might become God." "The only-begotten Son of God, wanting to make us sharers in his divinity, assumed our nature, so that he, made man, might make men gods." (CCC 460)

How did he do this? Jesus became like us in his human nature in all things but sin. He willingly suffered hunger, thirst, and physical pain like we do (indeed to a far greater extent). He also suffered excruciating emotional pains like being let down by his closest friends as he prayed in the Garden of Gethsemane, while another erstwhile friend was busy betraying him. He would also see his loving mother witness his crucifixion. Though Jesus suffered immensely at times, he possessed and displayed all the virtues[167] and the gifts of the Holy Spirit in the highest degree, and yet he most explicitly directed us to *love* God, neighbor, and self, as exemplified in his own life of *humility*—that is, in *gentleness* and *lowliness of heart.*

And how did Christ teach us the humility he bade us to learn from him? St. Thomas Aquinas, perhaps the Church's greatest theological "doctor" (i.e., "teacher," from the Latin *docere*—to teach) said Jesus was the greatest teacher of all, "the most excellent of teachers," who taught not through writing but in "that manner of teaching whereby His doctrine is imprinted on the hearts of His hearers," and "as one having power" *through the words and deeds of his life.*[168] So central is humility to Christ's teaching, and to the deeds of his life on earth, that St. Thomas would remind us of Augustine's insightful words that "almost the whole of Christian teaching is humility."[169]

Hopefully, we have gotten a glimpse of the truths of Augustine's words within these pages. If we fully unwrap Christian humility, we find within it the keys to growth in all virtues, to greater utilization of the Holy Spirit's gifts, greater mastery over sin. As we strive to climb the ladder and the mountain of humility, we mimic young Jesus, in his human nature, who "increased in wisdom and in stature, and in favor with God and man" (Luke 2:52).

A little less than two decades later, that beloved twelve-year-old boy who had been found by his parents in the Temple of Jerusalem had reached the fullness of maturity in wisdom and stature. He began sharing his good news of humility and love through his social ministry in the words and deeds of his life. The God-man, the King of Kings, chose not the rich, the powerful, or the learned as his friends and disciples but the likes of humble fishermen and a tax collector. He revealed to them the power and love of God for them and explained that in the kingdom of heaven "the last will be first, and the first last" (Matthew 20:16).

Indeed, as he explained to his disciples in his Sermon on the Mount, the poor in spirit, the mourners, the meek, those who hunger and thirst for righteousness, the merciful, the pure of heart, the peacemakers, and those who are persecuted for righteousness' sake (see Matthew 5:3–11) are the *blessed* ones whose rewards will be great. We see in all the Gospels how the vast majority of Jesus' words and deeds were carried out with and for simple, ordinary people, and some of them great sinners in dire need of his gospel of love. The beatitudes are built upon humility and love and are potentially accessible to all who would seek them out.

Just a few short years into his ministry, the child who had grown in favor with God and men became a man despised by many, especially the powerful who were threatened by his humble message, and he would willingly suffer an excruciating crucifixion for our sake.

Meekness Is Not Weakness

Still, Jesus' gentleness and meekness, his willingness to suffer, should never be confused with weakness or a lack of fortitude. True meekness is the properly measured use of one's powers.

We saw how Jesus overturned the money-changers' tables when they desecrated his Father's house (see Matthew 21:12–17; Mark 11:15–19; Luke 19:45–48; John 2:13–16), but he did not turn them to dust. Further, let's consider that fortitude does not mean that one does not fear, but that one overcomes his fears. During his prayers in the Garden of Gethsemane, foreseeing his passion and crucifixion, Jesus sweat blood (see Luke 22:44) in anguish, but he resolved to do his Father's will, regardless of the suffering it would bring him.

St. Thomas had provided other interesting insights on Christ's call to become meek and humble like him (see Matthew 11:29):

> And that which is said: Learn of me, because I am meek and humble of heart? For the whole New Law consists in two things: in meekness and humility. By meekness, a man is ordained to his neighbor. Hence, "O Lord, remember David, and all his meekness (Ps. 131.1).[170] By humility, he is ordained himself and to God. "Upon whom shall my spirit rest, but upon him that is quiet and humble" (Isa. 66:2).[171]

When David was meek, humble, and small, with God's grace he slew the giant Goliath and later became the king of God's chosen people. Jesus, "the son of David" (Matthew 1:1), conquered Satan and slew death through his meekness and humility. How humbling to think that Christ, the King, the Lord of all creation, came to us "taking the form of a servant" (Philippians 2:7) so that we should be no longer his servants but his friends (see John 15:15).

Of course, our greatest friend would willingly die for us at the peak of his wisdom and maturity as a man in his early thirties, and in doing so he continued to teach the most sublime lessons. St. Thomas More (1478–1535), himself a prisoner in the Tower of London and soon to be a martyr, noted that some martyrs are known for facing death fearlessly, sometimes even provoking it and accepting it with open arms. Yet he saw that Christ, the Lamb of God, provided the ultimate model for facing even death with gentleness and humility. As we have seen, in providing solace to the lonely, St. Thomas imagines these words of comfort from Christ:

> Let the brave man have his high-spirited martyrs, let him rejoice in imitating a thousand of them. But you, my timorous and feeble little sheep, be content to have me alone as your shepherd, follow my leadership; if you do not trust yourself, place your trust in me. See, I am walking ahead of you along this fearful road. Take hold of the border of my garment and you will feel going out from it a power which will stay your heart's blood from issuing in vain fears and will make your mind more cheerful, especially when you remember that you are following closely in my footsteps (and I am to be trusted and will not allow you to be tempted beyond what you can bear, but I will give together with the temptation a way out that you may be able to endure it).[172]

How Infinite Immensity Becomes Small for Us Every Day

Over two thousand years ago, through the miracle of the Incarnation, the infinite Word of God, omnipresent in his essence, presence, and power, humbled himself to become enclosed within his mother's womb. For nearly two thousand years, through the miracle of the Eucharist he gave us, Jesus has become small again for us, in a most mystical and intensely intimate way, every single day.

Some Christians speak of their "personal relationship" with Jesus Christ, and indeed what relationship could possibly be more important? On the surface, it could sound a bit like vainglorious name-dropping: "The Lord Jesus Christ? Oh yes, I know him well. In fact, he is a dear personal friend of mine!"

Digging deeper, the statement is rich in profound truths that speak of humility and love. Jesus did indeed come to call us not servants but friends, and to make us adoptive children of God. St. Thomas Aquinas says that while one of our great joys in heaven will be to gaze upon Jesus Christ face-to-face, Jesus offers us his friendship in the most unique way while we are still here on earth. Indeed, in the sacrament of the Eucharist, we find Christ present in a more real, profound, and mysterious way than he can be found anywhere else on earth.

Thomas makes crystal clear though multiple arguments from Scripture and the Church Fathers that the Body of Christ is in the sacrament of the Eucharist "in very truth" and not "only as in a figure or sign." He cites Berengarius of Tours (c. 999–1088) as the first to devise the heresy that Christ's body and blood are present in the Eucharist only as a spiritual sign (a belief now held by many non-Catholic Christians). Among many intriguing, moving defenses of Christ's real presence in the Eucharist, Thomas cites Matthew, John—and Aristotle![173]

Recall that Jesus told us, "No longer do I call you servants, for the servant does not know what his master is doing; but I have called you friends" (John 15:15). Aristotle writes that a "special feature of friendship" is "to live together with friends." Thomas notes Christ promised his bodily presence to us as a reward at the close of the age in Matthew 24:28: "Wherever the body is, there the eagles will be gathered together." Still, even during our pilgrimage on earth he provides us with his bodily presence through the Eucharist. "He says: 'He that eateth My flesh, and drinketh My blood, abideth in Me, and I in him.' Hence this sacrament is the sign of supreme charity, and the uplifter of our hope, from such familiar union of Christ with us."[174]

Thomas describes the miracle of transubstantiation, whereby in the sacrament of the Eucharist the *substance* of the bread and wine is changed into the Body, Blood, Soul, and Divinity, while the *accidents* of the bread and wine perceptible by our senses continue to remain.[175] As he noted in the first article of this question, "The presence of Christ's true body and blood in this sacrament cannot be detected by sense, nor understanding, but by faith alone, which rests upon Divine authority. Hence, on Luke 22:19: 'This is My body which shall be delivered up for you,' Cyril says: 'Doubt not whether this be true: but take rather the Saviour's words with faith; for since He is the Truth, He lieth not.'"[176]

Thomas reminds doubters of the Real Presence that while "every change made according to nature's laws is a formal change," God's power is unlimited, and "hence His action extends to the whole nature of being. Therefore He can work not only formal conversion, so that diverse forms succeed each other in the same subject; but also the change of all being, so that, to wit, the whole substance of one thing be changed into the whole substance of another" as "the whole substance of the bread is changed into the whole substance of Christ's body, and the whole substance of the wine into the whole substance of Christ's blood."[177]

Truly, while the miracle of Christ's sacramental real presence in the Eucharist—Body, Blood, Soul, and Divinity—far exceeds our capacity for complete understanding, it should inflame our sense of *humility* and *gratitude* that Christ would give himself to us in this way.

Indeed, the call to humility and our proclamation of it are ensconced in the prayers surrounding the Eucharist at Mass.

In the Mass, we proclaim before Holy Communion, "Lord, I am not worthy that you should enter under my roof, but only say the word and my soul shall be healed." In doing so, we humbly echo the words of the Roman centurion to Jesus: "Lord … I am not worthy to have you come under my roof … But say the word, and let my servant be healed" (Luke 7:6–7). What an astounding thing to ponder, that the Lord Jesus Christ should enter under the roof our mouth, so that we might be healed!

In the traditional Latin Mass, the priest prays aloud three times the words *"Domine, non sum dignus … Domine, non sum dignus … Domine, non sum dignus …"*—"Lord, I am not worthy … Lord, I am not worthy … Lord, I am not worthy." In fact, he does so twice. (I cannot help when I write these words to hear in my imagination the awe-inspiring, spine-tingling effect that occurs when our pastor chants these words so sonorously and sincerely.) Yet even though we are not worthy, the Lord chooses to give himself to us in this most amazingly intimate way. Indeed, after Communion, the priest prays that Christ's Body and Blood received in the Eucharist will *"adhaereat visceribus meis"* ("cleave to my innermost parts.")

"I Look at Him and He Looks At Me"

We need not be able even to begin to fathom with our minds the sublime mysteries of Christ's real presence in the Eucharist to feel his real presence in our hearts. Remembering Christ's call to be humble and gentle like him, who cannot help but to love the story told by the French parish priest who would one day be the patron saint of parish priests. St. John Vianney (1786–1859) saw an old man in his church one day just staring at the tabernacle. The holy priest asked what he was doing, and the old man responded, "I look at him and he looks at me." Could reverent contemplation of Christ be any humbler, gentler, or simpler?

Humility and Charity Yoke Joyfully Together in Christ

Jesus stated so clearly: "If you love me, you will keep my commandments" (John 14:15). Among his foremost commandments, along with love of God and neighbor as oneself, were to eat his flesh and drink his blood in the sacrament of the Eucharist, and to be gentle and lowly like him in the thoughts, words, and deeds of our everyday life.

Jesus told us that to learn how to become gentle and lowly like him, we must take up his yoke. He said that his yoke will provide rest for our souls, "For my yoke is easy, and my burden is light" (Matthew 11:30). What an amazing commandment—and promise, but what exactly did Christ mean by his yoke? This is truly worthy of employing our powers of understanding to their fullest, with the help of our Church's great Fathers and Doctors.

St. Thomas, in his *Commentary on the Gospel of St. Matthew*, notes that Christ's yoke replaces a yoke of sin with the yoke of the Gospel, citing, among others, St. Paul: "But thanks be to God, that you who were once slaves of sin ... having been set free from sin, have become slaves of righteousness" (Romans 6:17–18). The everlasting rest Christ's yoke will provide is "namely, the fulfillment of your desires."[178]

St. Thomas, in his *Catena Aurea* ("golden chain") on the Gospel of St. Matthew, cites theologians including St. Hilary of Poitiers (c. 315–367):

> And what is more pleasant than that yoke, what lighter than that burden? To be made better, to abstain from wickedness, to choose the good, and refuse the evil, to love all men, to hate none, to gain eternal things, not to be taken with things present, to be unwilling to do that to another which yourself would be pained to suffer.[179]

Consider further the words of Rabanus Maurus (c. 780–856):

> But how is Christ's yoke pleasant, seeing it was said above, "Narrow is the way which leadeth unto life?" That which is entered upon by a narrow entrance is in process of time made broad by the unspeakable sweetness of love. [180]

Finally, let's ponder the eloquent insights of Cistercian abbot St. Aelred of Rievaulx (c. 1110–1167):

> Yes, his yoke is easy and his burden light: therefore you will find rest for your souls. This yoke does not oppress but unites; this burden has wings, not weight. This yoke is charity. This burden is brotherly love.[181]

St. Hilary describes burdensome weights of sins and frustrated desires we cast away when we humbly take on Christ's yoke and follow him toward eternal bliss.

As a lifelong weight lifter myself, when I read Rabanus' words I think of the joke bodybuilders will play by flaring out their "lats" and holding wide their arms, pretending they are too big to fit through a doorway. We cannot get through a doorway or a narrow gate if we are puffed up, pretending that we are more than we are. Yet if we acknowledge our smallness, we can enter Christ's narrow gate, and then, over time, as we grow in our acceptance of his love, we will find that our road is both broad and sweet.

Finally, St. Aelred reveals that sharing in Christ's humility yokes us to Christ's love and joyfully shares that love with our neighbor. St. John Paul II writes at the beginning of his encyclical *Fides et Ratio* that "faith and reason are like two wings on which the human spirit rises to the contemplation of truth."[182] St. Aelred essentially tells us that humility and love provide the wings that will raise our souls, and someday our bodies, to heaven.

Humility's Holy Toolbox:

Talking with and Cleaving to Christ

1. **Prayer** – When we look at Christ, he looks at us. When we talk with Christ, he talks with us—if we are quiet and attentive enough to listen to the still, small voice of his Spirit (see 1 Kings 19:12). St. Thomas Aquinas himself, the Doctor of the Eucharist and theorist of transubstantiation, declared that he learned more through prayer than through all his years of study. Brother Reginald of Piperno, Thomas' closest friend, declared at Thomas' canonization proceedings, "When perplexed by a difficulty he would kneel and pray and then, on returning to his writing or dictation, he was accustomed to find that his thought had become so clear that it seemed to show him inwardly, as in a book, the words he needed."[183] As one Dominican commentator has noted, Thomas knew well that "in prayer only do we stand face to face with the Teacher ... and without whose assistance and light we can learn nothing."[184]

   Of course, Christ himself showed us how to pray and even gave us the words to say. Virtually every saint has prayed countless times the Our Father prayer Jesus gave us (Matthew 6:9–13). It assisted their wonderful growth in humility and will stimulate the growth of our own humility too (not matter how small it might be!).[185]

2. **The sacrament of the Eucharist** – St. Thomas, like all the great theologians before him and since, recognized the Eucharist as the sacrament of charity or love. It is in this sacrament that Christ gives himself to us, the friends that he died for. If any sacrament should help us grow in humility, to become more humble and gentle like Christ, it is the Eucharist above all others. Our *Catechism* tells us plainly that the Eucharist is "the source and summit of the Christian life" (CCC 1324). How fitting that Blessed Pier Giorgio Frassati and his friends loved to receive the Eucharist while hiking high in the mountains. The Eucharist is there to help raise us all to the heights of St. Anselm's mountain of humility as well. Let us always receive the Eucharist with awe and profound humility. It is true that *we are not worthy* that God himself should come under the roofs of our mouths to cleave to our inmost parts, but he lovingly chooses to do so for us.

Chapter 7 Summary and Reflections

We saw how the infinite Word of God chose in the Incarnation to become as "small" for us as a baby within his mother's womb by taking on a human nature (in addition to his divine nature) for us. Jesus Christ ascended to the top of humility's ladder at the peak of humility's mountain.

Christ's ladder was the Cross and his mountain was called "the place of a skull," *Golgotha* in Hebrew, *Calvary* in Latin (see Matthew 27:33; Mark 15:22; Luke 23:33; John 19:17). We saw too that though he ascended into heaven, he continues to abide with us, like good friends do, even before we reach heaven's gates. He becomes "small" for us sacramentally again and again at every Mass when humble fruits of the earth, mere bread and wine, are transubstantiated into his Body, Blood, Soul, and Divinity so that they might heal our souls.

- We should ask ourselves each morning how *today* we can place upon our backs and necks the yoke of humility and love he has prepared for every one of us if we are prepared to accept its light and sweet burden.

- But what about *right now*? Christ bade us to show our love for him, by keeping his commandments. He told us that "as you did it to one of the least of these my brethren, you did it to me" (Matthew 25:40). As soon as you set this book aside, can you think of some small way to humble yourself and treat the next person you meet as though you were interacting with Jesus himself, perhaps offering a warm smile to a stranger or a firm hug and kind words to a family member?

Humility Lived Saint Story #7

Our Blessed Mother Mary

But the Blessed Virgin is an example of all virtues. Thus you find in her a model of humility. ("Behold the handmaid of the Lord," [see Luke 1:38] and further on, "He hath regarded the humility of His handmaid" [see Luke 1:48].)[186]

—St. Thomas Aquinas

Oh, how sweet is Mary's image! See, what care artists take to make it surpass in beauty those of other saints. See how solicitous are the faithful to show it due veneration. Churches are adorned with her pictures that our thoughts may dwell devoutly on her. In heaven we shall behold not her image in marble or on canvas, but her own most beautiful soul and body. We shall gaze on her sweet countenance, and its beauty shall ravish us throughout eternity.[187]

—St. Albert the Great

The Blessed Virgin Mary was given the greatest gifts any human being had ever received. Not only did God grant her an immaculate conception, creating her free from all sin, he filled her with all of his graces. Indeed, theologians like St. Albert and

St. Thomas said when the archangel Gabriel hailed Mary as "full of grace," he meant it quite literally. Albert and Thomas said the Blessed Virgin Mary was filled with grace in "super-abundance." Indeed, in his sermon on the Hail Mary prayer, Thomas said Mary was full of grace in three ways:[188]

1) *Her soul was full of grace.* There was no place for sin within Mary's soul, which brimmed over with every virtue and gift of the Holy Spirit. Thus, she is a perfect human model for every virtue, and indeed, as we saw, Thomas' first example was the virtue of humility.

2) *Her body was full of grace.* All saints have souls that are holy, but "the soul of the Blessed Virgin was so full of grace that it overflowed into her flesh, fitting it for the conception of God's Son."[189] Indeed, saints like Albert wrote extensively about how this grace gave Mary an incomparable physical beauty as well. We saw one example in our opening quotation. He also wrote eloquently about her holy beauty in commenting on the Song of Solomon where the question is raised: "Who is this that looks forth like the dawn, fair as the moon, bright as the sun?" (Song of Solomon 6:10). Albert calls Mary the dawn who is followed by the sunlight of Christ. She is "the dawn of all grace unto our glory—the dawn rising in the fullness of grace and yet growing even into the perfection of day."[190]

3) *Humanity receives grace through her.* Thomas elaborates: "It is, indeed, a great thing that any one saint has so much grace that it is conducive to the salvation of many; but it is most wondrous to have so much grace as to suffice for the salvation of all mankind."[191] (Hence, the Church honors Mary with the title Mediatrix of All Graces.)

How interesting that when we meet this human being graced beyond all others, hailed and honored by an angel, her words are suffused with humility, calling herself but the Lord's handmaid and consenting fully to whatever God wills. This she did throughout her entire life on earth, a life of humility, service, love, and suffering for her son and for all of us too. We have relatively few of her words while on earth, but perhaps her most straightforward pearl of wisdom to all of us was her advice to the servants at the wedding feast of Cana regarding her holy son: "Do whatever he tells you" (John 2:5).

Mary, ever humble, would go on to receive many honorific titles as the centuries passed, including recognition that she is the Mother of the Church and the Queen of Heaven, and highest of all, the Mother of God. Indeed, besides Jesus himself, was there ever greater proof of Jesus' proclamation that "whoever humbles himself will be exalted" (Matthew 23:12) than the case of his own Blessed Mother?[192]

Conclusion

LIVING OUR OWN
"HUMILITY LIVED SAINT STORIES"

*Humility is, then, a most practical and sanctifying
virtue; it extends to the whole man, and aids us in
the practice of all the other virtues.*[193]

—Adolphe Tanquery

It is no longer I who live, but Christ who lives in me.

—Galatians 2:20

We have looked at humility through many lenses throughout this book,
lenses that revealed it as the foundation of virtue, as the great conqueror
of pride and all its sinful brood, as a perfection of soul achieved through
God's grace and our efforts by a succession of steps, degrees, or levels, and
as a virtue that Christ specifically bade us take up if we are to learn from
him, follow him, and allow him to live in us. Hopefully, our intellects have
found many perhaps unsuspected characteristics and qualities of humility

that we can think over and incorporate as we strive to assemble some semblance of humility in our bodies and souls over time.

We have come to see how closely humility is tied to the *truth*, the truth about ourselves, our neighbors and God. We have come to realize the many ways humility can lead to both *earthly* and *heavenly* rewards. Of course, to come to know and love the truth and to obtain lowly humility's great rewards, we must get busy and put humility into action every day of our lives, just as we saw so many saints did.

Hopefully, you have found the anecdotes about the saints and the Humility Lived Saint Stories of interest and use. The saints show us so well how to turn abstract virtues into concrete, lived realities. As Fr. Tanquerey has said, humility is "practical." Humility works and gets holy jobs done. Indeed, he noted humility is "sanctifying," too. To sanctify is to set apart and make holy. The saints did this with their lives, and every one of *us* is also called to be a saint someday in heaven by accepting God's graces to sanctify our own lives and to live as Christ for others, regardless of where we live or whatever our vocation may be.

Now, probably few of us will become canonized saints, but know that the heavenly communion of saints is brimming over with souls who were everyday people from all times, nations, and walks of life. These saints, people we have never heard of, strove to live humble, holy lives and ended up in heaven. So, I will end with some questions for every one of us, each of us a potential saint in the making.

If there were someday to be an essay written in honor of your own acts of humility (or perhaps more likely a discussion among your surviving friends and loved ones), which of these actions would be written about or discussed? Can you think of any such acts you have performed? (Don't worry, I am not asking you to be boastful here, just honest.) Think too of the humbling, loving acts that you have left undone. Regardless of your answers, ask yourself what you might do with your time left on earth *to practice true humility from this moment forward*?

Is there some sin you must own up to before you can really join in battle? Is there some virtue you need to admit that you lack and then seek God's grace to help you get out there and get? Do you need to work on humility by changing your habits regarding particular thoughts, deeds, or gestures? Do you like to show off your material things or draw attention to yourself with gaudy clothing and the like? How do you treat the downtrodden and lonely—those who may feel more lowly and unworthy of love and respect? Do you look the other way, or, like Blessed Pier Giorgio Frassati, go out of your way to seek them out and cherish them? Do you bristle at insults or personal slights? If so, could you possibly muster the humility to do some kind act for the next person who insults or slights you? (Not easy to do, but a prayer to St. Martin de Porres might help!)

In any event, I do hope you will never forget Christ's call to become "gentle and lowly in heart" like him. As the Doctor of Grace, St. Augustine sums it up so well: *"Almost the whole of Christian teaching is humility."*

Humility's Maintenance Manual

A FIFTY-ITEM USER GUIDE

We have come to the close of our humble assembly manual for humility, but there are a few last things we should consider. Let's use this maintenance manual by following these fifty procedures as often as possible, so that we can keep our humility functioning properly (and stay in compliance with its eternal lifetime God-given warranty.)

1. Remember that humility is the *"new smart"* (and has always been the old one, too). Admit to yourself how much remains to be learned about things that matter much.

2. Be willing to say *"I don't know,"* even if asked about something in which you're considered an expert.

   I recall years ago seeing one of our very best modern Catholic authors on a television show being interviewed about his newest book. The host flashed a particular image on the screen and asked him exactly what it meant. The author did not miss a beat. He smiled, chuckled to himself, and replied, "I don't remember that one!" How refreshingly honest and humble!

3. *Don't pretend* to know what you don't. Monkey around like that and you may end up all wet.

4. *Know yourself.* Seek to know the truth about your own strengths and weaknesses by openness to feedback and criticism. Then go out and *strengthen your strengths* and *shore up your weaknesses.*

5. Cultivate docility by finding *wise people* to teach you and guide you (whether in person or through their writings, media presentations, etc.).

6. Cultivate docility by recognizing that virtually *every person* you meet may have lessons to teach you about humility and other important things in life.

7. If you find yourself among humble people, do not be afraid to be a *copycat.*

8. Give due honor to those whom God called to *Holy Orders* in the priesthood to help guide us toward lives of humility and love.

9. Seek to grow in humility and in the intellectual virtues by paying close attention when they are mentioned or lived out in *the stories of Scripture or your other spiritual reading.*

10. *If any of you lacks wisdom, ask God* in good faith, and he will gladly give it to you. (Sound a little familiar? OK, so I borrowed a bit from St. James 1:5–6).

11. Do not count yourself better or more entitled than anyone else. *Give every person his or her rightful due in the spirit of justice,* just as you would expect others to give you what's rightfully yours.

12. Stay grounded in the humility of our sinful human nature, but from that firm base, reach for the stars in heaven in the spirit of *magnanimity,* recognizing God's call toward spiritual greatness and remembering Christ's gift of the strength through which we can do great things.

13. Whatever talents God gave you, don't employ a false humility (perhaps disguising a weak pusillanimity) as an excuse to bury them under the ground. *Multiply them and share them with others for the greater glory of God.*

14. The next time the dinner platter comes your way, take the *smaller portion* of meat or the one that's a little too grizzled.

15. If you don't do this already, when the holidays come around, *let the seniors, the children, and everyone else get in the food line before you.* (It

took years for me, but due to the relentless teasing of my brother, who has struggled throughout his entire life to help me grow in humility, he who was first is now usually last.)

16. Don't jump to the head of the table. When you are invited to a meal, *go and sit in the lowest place.* (That one sure sounds familiar. Oh yes, Luke 14:8–11).

17. The next time you are at some kind of social event, build your humility and patience by *striking up a friendly conversation with a person who tends to get on your nerves.*

18. *Always give God his rightful due to the best of your ability.* Keep him foremost in your thoughts. Pray to him. Go to Mass. Live out both internal and external acts of the virtue of religion.

19. *Honor your father and your mother!* (Now that one sounds familiar, too. Oh yes, Commandment 4. See Exodus 20:12, Deuteronomy 5:16, and Ephesians 6:2). After all, piety serves justice, and humility undergirds both.

20. *Give thanks* to God for all he has given you and show gratitude to those people who do you a good turn. Thank them and spread the good word to others about their generosity.

21. *Acknowledge the God-given dignity of every person you happen to meet,* be it at the office, in the elevator, at the gym, or in the grocery store. A simple hello or even a smile tells that person you know that he or she matters.

22. Let humility make you more *prudent.* Remember important lessons you've learned from the wise in the past so you too might act wisely in similar situations.

23. Don't let a false sense of humility keep you from employing your powers of *reasoning and understanding* to their fullest to make the most prudent decisions, whether they are important life decisions or the little moral decisions we make every day of our lives.

24. Grow in *foresight* at predicting the likely outcomes of your actions by continually striving to grasp your personal strengths and weaknesses

as you progress through life (and hopefully as you climb the ladder and mountain of humility).

25. Think back from time to time to your *Confirmation*. Recall and unwrap those seven gifts of the Holy Spirit. Hop on their spiritual ladder at the first rung of fear of the Lord and allow God's Spirit to help you climb, with Samson-like strength, all the way to wisdom at the top.

26. It doesn't have to be March 17th to *pray to St. Patrick of Ireland*, the self-proclaimed sinner whom many declared "worthless," that we too might be graced with humble hearts that do not fear to accomplish great things in Christ's honor.

27. Seek to grow in your knowledge of the *Faith*. Read Scripture, become familiar with the *Catechism*, and also include new and old Catholic spiritual classics in your personal library. (If you have spare time after that, you might want to get started on St. Thomas' *Summa Theologica*. Be warned, though: it weighs in at over one-million-and-a-half words, as many as you would find in about two dozen books of this book's size!)

28. Drink from an eternal spring. Of course, it is *hope* that springs eternal. Cherish hope as a great gift of God, a gift that can bring us to heaven one day. And cherish it in the spirit of humility, neither presuming that we can lift ourselves to heaven by our own bootstraps nor despairing, through a twisted kind of pride, that *our* sins are so magnificently grave that even God's divine mercy cannot forgive them.

29. *Enlarge and crank up your furnace of love!* Being humble in no way excuses us from the obligation that we've got a lot of loving to do. Christ told us to love God with all we are and our neighbor as our self. So, let's turn up that heat to warm strangers and even our enemies, and make sure that those we live with are always kept nice and warm.

30. *Throw some flowers* at God and neighbor. (Not necessarily real ones, but if you do, little flowers work best.) Imitate St. Thérèse and make the humblest acts of your daily life into bouquets (not buckets) of love.

31. Sorry about this one, but *go clean your family's toilets*! (There are prideful and humbling little stories behind this one.)

    Before my first book came out, I never tired of telling my wife, tongue partially in cheek, that I was going to be a "world-famous author." After the book was published, Kathy had a special tee shirt made for me with the book's cover image and big letters that spelled out WFA (as in "World Famous Author.") I must admit I've never once worn that shirt outside of the house. Still, from time to time, especially before we host some kind of get-together, Kathy will tell me or ask me (it's hard to tell the difference) to clean our bathrooms, including the toilets. I will ask her (just for fun) what readers might think if a WFA, such as myself, were seen scrubbing down toilets. Without fail, she gives me a wry look, hands me the cleaners and brush, and reminds me that she will be checking to make sure I did it right.

32. Even if you should be as old as I am, take a lesson from twenty-four-year-old Blessed Pier Giorgio Frassati. The next time you go to a social gathering, *keep your eyes peeled for a person who appears lonely or sad, go over there, strike up a conversation, and treat that person as gently and humbly as Christ would* (and don't hesitate to share a moderately mirthful laugh or two, too).

33. Don't let envy win out over humility. If someone else should win some contest, some honor, or some promotion you were after, *be quick to congratulate* that person if you can and pray that God will continue to shower his blessings upon him or her. If you lose in a team sport, go shake the winners' hands (and vice versa, if you win). If you lose in some kind of one-on-one athletic competition, go and raise the victor's hand in front of the crowd (and if you should win, duly acknowledge the other guy or gal who did not win this time).

34. You wouldn't happen to be a professional bodybuilder or runway model, would you? Well, even if you just like to admire your clothing or make sure your hair looks all right, join the cause to *call back vainglory* and replace it with humility by resisting the urge to steal a look when you happen to pass by a mirror.

35. *Go to confession* when you have committed injustices or any other sins. True confession requires a humility that God himself rewards, not only by remitting our sins but by reopening the free flow of his graces into our souls.

36. If you would like to climb the ladder of humility, do what St. Benedict (and Christ) bade us do: *fear and love God* and *keep his commandments* (especially those ten special ones God gave Moses and the great two that Jesus spelled out for us).

37. St. Benedict has made clear that you cannot climb humility's ladder without thinking *humble thoughts*.

38. You will get stuck on the ladder's bottom rungs if you don't *humble your willful desires* and strive to employ St. Maximilian Kolbe's super simple algebra: $W = w$.

39. *Keep a close watch on your tongue and don't dominate conversations.* Here's a little more simple algebra to try: $x = y/z$, where x equals the amount of time you talk, y equals the total time of the conversation, and z equals the number of participants.

    For example, if a conversation is about twenty minutes long and there are four people talking, try to keep your allotment to five minutes or less. (You need not use a stopwatch, of course, but hopefully you'll find this a rough and simple rule of thumb—or better yet, rule of tongue.) Also, be sure sometimes to let the other guy or gal get in the last word.

40. Everyone's entitled to his opinion, *but that does not mean you should always express yours!* Sometimes, keep silent and listen to multiple sides of an argument. You may well find there are things you thought you knew but you didn't, and the opinion you would have expressed if you'd rushed would have been an opinion you'd come to regret.

41. *Keep your gestures modest and humble.* If you spend too much time patting down your hair, sucking in your gut, flexing your muscles, or pulling out your phone for a selfie, you may well fall right off humility's ladder or even slide off humility's cliff.

42. Remember that *climbing the mountain of humility is no easy task.* It is so much easier to slide down into the valley of pride, but remember, that's where the wild and beastly things are. Ask God, and he will provide you with all the mountaineering equipment you need, and he will even provide you with earthly and heavenly guides to make sure that you reach the summit.

43. Think about people whom you let irritate you and ponder what kinds of *hidden gifts God may have given them.* What hardships might they have overcome? What good deeds might they do about which you have no clue? This will help you "in humility count others better than yourselves" (Philippians 2:3).

44. The next time a person *insults you or harms you,* think of some way you can perform a small act of kindness toward them, even if you do it anonymously. (Either way, you can be sure, St. Martin de Porres will look down upon you and smile.)

45. Enjoy your cheese, but without a drop of *whine.* Humility does not shy away from striving to make bad situations better when it can, but complaining, grumbling, and whining of any sort are not in humility's vocabulary. So the next time you catch yourself whining, quickly put a cork in it!

46. *Pray sometime to St. Humilitas.* If you ask her, she'll undoubtedly ask God to give you your own share of the humility she is named for.

47. Speaking of holy women, *let the Blessed Mother be our model of perfect humility and our go-to intercessor for humility as the Mediatrix of All Graces.* Think about Mary, carefully read her words, and observe her actions in the Gospels and the book of Acts. Then pray the Hail Mary or any number of beautiful Marian prayers before speaking to her simply and lovingly as any child does with his or her mother.

48. *Look at Christ and let him look at you.* Embrace Christ in the Gospels and in the Eucharist. Sit there and look upon him in Eucharistic Adoration or even before a crucifix or other piece of holy art within your own home. Let him cleave to your innermost parts. Let him

show you how to become gentle, humble, and loving like him so that you and your loved ones will one day come to live in the mansions he's prepared for you.

49. *Embrace your role as abbot, abbess, monk, or nun, as the case may be, even if only within the domestic church of your own household.* While it's probably *not* a good idea to ask your spouse or children to strive to become humble like you, it's always a good idea to strive to teach by example, sharing the gospel of humility in your actions more than in your words.

50. *Get down on your knees and pray that God will shower you in humility.* Speak simply in your own words or craft your own prayer if you are so moved. In the meanwhile, please feel free to try out the one I crafted in the pages that follow (as usual, patterned after the model of St. Thomas Aquinas) or the beautiful, beloved traditional Litany of Humility that brings this book to its close.

Godspeed to you and yours

on your journey up God's heavenly mountain

of holy, happy humility!

A Prayer to Acquire Humility

O humble and most exalted Lord,

beginning and end

of all that is true and good,

Grant us the grace to savor humility,

that we may seek to learn from you how to be gentle and lowly.

Illuminate our minds to relish the truth

through the intellectual powers you gave us in your
likeness and image.

Grant unto us

knowledge of our place in the hierarchy of being,

understanding that penetrates to the heart of your love
for us as we are,

and the wisdom to grow in humility during our
brief sojourn on earth.

Raise us up to fly high with your four holy cardinals:

fortitude to strive for great things with the aid of
your mighty arm,

temperance to desire only what is truly fitting and best,

justice to give each person his or her rightful due,
as we expect for ourselves,

and the prudence to put humility in action in the acts
of our everyday lives.

Infuse into our hearts and souls

humble faith to believe in you and to believe you,

humble hope to join you someday in heaven by accepting your
eternal life-giving grace,

and humble charity to love our true selves, our neighbor
just as much, and you above all.

Grant us your strength to humbly seek your aid

to dethrone the "queen of the vices," humility's
chief nemesis of pride,

to lift our drooping branches bowed down by sevens sins and
point them again to heaven,

to rein in our natural gluttony and lust through your
supernatural power,

to feel greedy only for your presence,

to route wrath by remembering our neighbor's weakness
(and our own),

to send sloth slithering away by dedicating our hearts, minds,
and souls to you,

to end envy by recognizing that our neighbors were
also created for joy,

to break vainglory's cracked mirror so that we might see
ourselves as we are

face-to-face on earth, so that we may one day see you
face-to-face in heaven.

Help hoist us up the ladder of humility,

purify our minds with humble thoughts,

ennoble our deeds, so that we may willingly serve
the true interests of others,

and sanctify our gestures, so sweet rays of humility will shine
forth from our faces and limbs.

Be our guide up humility's mountain,

so that we might grow in our knowledge of our own faults,

feel true contrition over them,

openly admit and confess them,

hope that our neighbor believes them,

patiently endure the enumeration of our faults,

be willingly treated as a lowly person,

and rest upon the mountain's peak enjoying the fact that others know us as we are.

Most of all, sweet Savior,

let us come to you like the children you so freely welcomed,

that we might sit at your feet listening like Martha's sister, Mary,

that we might recline upon your breast like your beloved disciple, John,

that we might learn firsthand your lessons of gentleness, humility, and love,

and carry those lessons out into the world to every person we meet.

We pray in humble gratitude

to you who have fashioned us from the lowly earth

that we might someday spend eternity with you, the angels, and saints in heaven.

Amen.[194]

The Litany of Humility

O Jesus, meek and humble of heart,
Make my heart like yours.

From self-will, deliver me, O Lord.

From the desire of being esteemed, deliver me, O Lord.

From the desire of being loved, deliver me, O Lord.

From the desire of being extolled, deliver me, O Lord.

From the desire of being honored, deliver me, O Lord.

From the desire of being praised, deliver me, O Lord.

From the desire of being preferred to others, deliver me, O Lord.

From the desire of being consulted, deliver me, O Lord.

From the desire of being approved, deliver me, O Lord.

From the desire to be understood, deliver me, O Lord.

From the desire to be visited, deliver me, O Lord.

From the fear of being humiliated, deliver me, O Lord.

From the fear of being despised, deliver me, O Lord.

From the fear of suffering rebukes, deliver me, O Lord.

From the fear of being calumniated, deliver me, O Lord.

From the fear of being forgotten, deliver me, O Lord.

From the fear of being ridiculed, deliver me, O Lord.

From the fear of being suspected, deliver me, O Lord.

From the fear of being wronged, deliver me, O Lord.

From the fear of being abandoned, deliver me, O Lord.

From the fear of being refused, deliver me, O Lord.

That others may be loved more than I,
Lord, grant me the grace to desire it.

That, in the opinion of the world, others may increase
and I may decrease,
Lord, grant me the grace to desire it.

That others may be chosen and I set aside,
Lord, grant me the grace to desire it.

That others may be praised and I go unnoticed,
Lord, grant me the grace to desire it.

That others may be preferred to me in everything,
Lord, grant me the grace to desire it.

That others may become holier than I, provided that
I may become as holy as I should,
Lord, grant me the grace to desire it.

At being unknown and poor,
Lord, I want to rejoice.

At being deprived of the natural perfections of body and mind,
Lord, I want to rejoice.

When people do not think of me,
Lord, I want to rejoice.

When they assign to me the meanest tasks,
Lord, I want to rejoice.

When they do not even deign to make use of me,
Lord, I want to rejoice.

When they never ask my opinion,
Lord, I want to rejoice.

When they leave me at the lowest place,
Lord, I want to rejoice.

When they blame me in season and out of season,
Lord, I want to rejoice.

Blessed are those who suffer persecution for justice's sake,
For theirs is the kingdom of heaven.

Amen. [195]

Notes

1   Fr. Cajetan Mary da Bergamo, *Humility of Heart*, trans. Herbert Cardinal Vaughan (Charlotte, NC: TAN Books, 2011), 1.

2   Aquinas, *Summa Theologica* II-II.161.5.

3   Henri Joly, *The Psychology of the Saints* (Fort Collins, CO: Roman Catholic Books, n.d.), 58.

4   Joly, 58.

5   "Counsels and Reminiscences of Soeur Thérèse, the Little Flower of Jesus," in *The Story of a Soul (L'Histoire d'une Âme): The Autobiography of St. Thérèse of Lisieux; With Additional Writings and Sayings of St. Thérèse*, ed. David McClamrock (2005), ccel.org.

6   "To Scatter Flowers," in "Selected Poems of Soeur Thérèse, The Little Flower of Jesus," in *The Story of a Soul*, ed. David McClamrock, ccel.org.

7   Therese is a patroness of France, Russia, sufferers of diseases including tuberculosis, those who have lost their parents, and indeed, most fittingly, of gardeners and florists!

8   Edward D. Hess and Katherine Ludwig, *Humility Is the New Smart: Rethinking Human Excellence in the Smart Machine Age* (Oakland, CA: Berrett-Koehler Publishers, Inc., 2017), 7.

9   Hess and Ludwig, 59.

10   Christopher Peterson and Martin E. P. Seligman, *Character Strengths and Virtues: A Handbook and Classification* (New York: Oxford University Press, 2004), 436.

11   Dietrich von Hildebrand, *Humility: Wellspring of Virtue* (Manchester, NH: Sophia Institute Press, 1990), 5.

12   Peterson and Seligman, 436.

13   Hess and Ludwig, *Humility Is the New Smart*, 7, 8.

14   Von Hildebrand, *Humility*, 8.

15 Von Hildebrand, 55.

16 da Bergamo, *Humility of Heart*, 1.

17 Andrew Murray, *Humility: The Beauty of Holiness* (Abbotsford, WI: Aneko, 2016), 11.

18 The Hebrew word for wisdom, *chokmah*, is grammatically feminine (so is Greek *sophia*). Hence wisdom is often spoken of as a woman, but this is only a personification, following on the fact that the noun, as we said, is *grammatically* feminine. Grammatical gender has nothing whatsoever to do with the real biological sexes of male and female.

19 The Rev. R. Garrigou-Lagrange, *The Three Ages of the Interior Life: Prelude of Eternal Life*, trans. Sister M. Timothea Doyle (Rockford, IL: TAN, 1989), 2:72.

20 Thomists are philosophers and theologians who base their philosophical and theological teachings upon the foundation of the writings of St. Thomas Aquinas. Fr. Garrigou-Lagrange was among the most respected and revered of twentieth-century Thomists. While he gladly endorsed truths espoused by other thinkers, he strove to adhere to the fundamental principles of St. Thomas as closely as he possibly could, since he considered them fundamental truths.

21 Truth from the human perspective is the correspondence between reality and our understanding of it, conformity between thing and thought. Not only do created things conform or correspond to God's thought, but "His act of understanding is the measure and cause of every other being and of every other intellect." Truth does not merely exist *in* God as it can in us, but "He is truth itself, and the sovereign and first truth" (Aquinas, *Summa Theologica* I.16.5). For us, thinking does not make it so. For God, it does!

22 Aquinas, *Summa Theologica* I-II.49.2.

23 "The Life and Works of Thomas Aquinas," in *Albert & Thomas: Selected Writings*, ed. and trans. Simon Tugwell, O.P. (New York: Paulist, 1988), 202–203. The little boy's "taste for books apparently antedated his ability to read!"

24 See Thomas Aquinas, *The Aquinas Catechism: A Simple Explanation of the Catholic Faith by the Church's Greatest Theologian*, with a foreword by Ralph McInerny (Manchester, NH: Sophia Institute Press, 2000).

25   Quoted in Leo XIII, *Aeterni Patris* (August 4, 1879), 17, vatican.va.

26   Aquinas, *Summa Theologica* II-II.8.1.

27   Aquinas, II-II.49.1.

28   Aristotle, *Rhetoric,* in Jonathan Barnes, ed. *The Complete Works of Aristotle,* vol. 2, (Princeton, NJ: Princeton University Press, 1984), 2213–2214 (book 2, chapter 12).

29   Rick Warren, *The Purpose Driven Life* (Grand Rapids, MI: Zondervan, 2012), 262; emphasis altered.

30   Aquinas, *Summa Theologica* I.1.5.

31   Aquinas, II-II.161.1.

32   Aquinas, I-II.57.2.

33   St. Francis de Sales, *Introduction to the Devout Life: A Popular Abridgement* (Rockford, IL: TAN, 1990), 134.

34   "It Ain't What You Don't Know That Gets You Into Trouble. It's What You Know for Sure That Just Ain't So," Quote Investigator (website), accessed December 17, 2021, quoteinvestigator.com.

35   With thanks to my editor for pointing out the recent documentary *The Social Dilemma,* directed by Jeff Orlowski (Exposure Labs, 2020), which makes facts like these crystal clear from the mouths of key figures who developed social media and Internet search engines.

36   Pope St. Gregory the Great, *The Homilies on the Prophet Ezekiel,* II.7.7. St. Robert Bellarmine (1542–1621) also explicitly compared the seven gifts to a ladder, the bottom step resting on the earth with fear of the Lord, and the top step touching heaven through the spirit of wisdom.

37   John of St. Thomas, *The Gifts of the Holy Ghost* (New York: Sheed and Ward, 1951), 208. I address this topic in my book *The Seven Gifts of the Holy Spirit: Every Spiritual Warrior's Guide to God's Invincible Gifts* (Manchester: NH: Sophia Institute Press, 2016), 36–37.

38   Blessed Raymond of Capua, *The Life of Saint Catherine of Siena* (Charlotte, NC: Saint Benedict Press, 2006), 54. (See Exodus 3:14.)

39   Aquinas, *Summa Theologica* II-II.9.2.

40   Aquinas, II-II.8.1.

41   Aquinas, II-II.9.2.

42   Aquinas, II-II.45.3.

43   Aquinas, *Summa Theologica* II-II.45.2; emphasis added. (Think
      perhaps of the sweetness of the *sap* of certain trees—especially the
      maple!)

44   *The Aquinas Prayer Book: The Prayers and Hymns of St. Thomas
      Aquinas,* ed. and trans. Robert Anderson and Johann Moser
      (Manchester, NH: Sophia Institute, 2000), 37.

45   *Aquinas Prayer Book*, 43.

46   John Paul II, "Science and Faith in the Search for Truth," address to
      teachers and university students in Cologne Cathedral (November 15,
      1980), catholicculture.org.

47   St. Albert, quoted in *The Fathers of the Church: Mediaeval
      Continuation*, ed. Gregory F. LaNave et. al., vol. 9, *Albert the Great:
      Questions Concerning Aristotle's* On Animals, trans. Irven M. Resnick
      and Kenneth F. Kitchell, Jr. (Washington, DC: Catholic University of
      America Press, 2008), 351.

48   From Albert's commentary on the Gospel of Matthew 13:35, quoted in
      Paul Murray, *The New Wine of Dominican Spirituality: A Drink Called
      Happiness* (New York: Burns and Oates, 2006), 93.

49   Joachim Sighart, *Albert the Great, of the Order of Friar-Preachers:
      His Life and Scholastic Labours*, trans. T.A. Dixon (London: R.
      Washbourne, 1876), 370, books.google.com.

50   For readers who might like to dig deeper into the lives of our featured
      saints I'll provide a recommended source or two for each one. For
      St. Albert, if you will forgive me, it will be a book that I wrote myself.
      I've written only one full-length biography of a saint, and I chose St.
      Albert, Thomas Aquinas' teacher, because there had not been a new
      biography for lay readers in over fifty years at the time I was writing.
      Here it is: Kevin Vost, *St. Albert the Great: Champion of Faith and
      Reason* (Charlotte, NC: TAN Books, 2011).

51   Aristotle, *Eudemian Ethics* 2.1220a.

52   Aquinas, *Summa Theologica* I-II. 58.2.

53   "Specific Phobia," National Institute of Mental Health (website), accessed December 20, 2021, nimh.nih.gov.

54   Here's a short, simple article if you'd care to start learning a bit more about this technique: Elissa Habinski, "Shame Attacks," The Albert Ellis Institute, accessed December 20, 2021, albertellis.org.

55   Diogenes Laertius, *Lives of Eminent Philosophers* 7.1.

56   Epictetus, *Discourses*, 2.13.

57   Aquinas, *Summa Theologica* II-II.123.3.

58   Aquinas, II-II.129.1.

59   Aquinas, II-II.133.1.

60   *Alles kann auch anders sein*—"Everything can also be different."

61   Aquinas, *Summa Theologica* II-II.161.1.

62   Aquinas, II-II.161.2.

63   Aquinas, II-II.123.6.

64   *The Dialogue of St. Catherine of Siena*, trans. Algar Thorold (Charlotte, NC: St. Benedict Press, 2006), 17.

65   Blessed Raymond of Capua, *The Life of St. Catherine of Siena*, trans. George Lamb (Charlotte, NC: TAN, 2011), 121.

66   From Cicero's *On Duties* 1.7, as cited in Aquinas, *Summa Theologica* II-II.58.12.

67   From Aristotle's *Nichomachean Ethics* 5.1, as cited in the same article of the *Summa* as above.

68   Aquinas, *Summa Theologica* II-II.161.5.

69   Aquinas, II-II.161.5.

70   St. Thomas Aquinas, *Commentary on Aristotle's* Nicomachean Ethics, trans. C.I. Litzinger (Notre Dame, IN: Dumb Ox Books, 1993), 366.

71   Aquinas, *Summa Theologica*, II-II.49.3.

72   Aquinas, II-II.51 (prologue).

73   Aquinas, II-II.139.1

74   Aquinas, II-II.123.4.

75   Here is a hint: Samson refers to "the seven locks of my head"
      (Judges 16:13).

76   For this analysis, see Bonaventure, *Works of St. Bonaventure*:
      Collations on the Seven Gifts of the Holy Spirit, trans. Zachary Hayes
      (St. Bonaventure, NY: Franciscan Institute Publications, 2008),
      especially page 113. I discuss this in my book *The Seven Gifts of the
      Holy Spirit.*

77   Aquinas, *Summa Theologica* II-II.161.2.

78   As cited in Aquinas, *Summa Theologica*, Supp.89.2. The Latin Bible
      translation employs the word "*pauperibus,*" which translates to "the
      poor." The Revised Standard Version–Second Catholic Edition reads:
      "He does not keep the wicked alive, but gives the afflicted their right."

79   Aquinas, *Summa Theologica* Supp.89.2.

80   John of St. Thomas, *The Gifts of the Holy Ghost,* trans. Dominic
      Hughes (New York: Sheed & Ward, 1951), 161.

81   *Aquinas Prayer Book*, 33, 35.

82   Excerpted from St. Alphonsus Liguori's "Prayer for the Gifts of the
      Holy Spirit," posted at Catholic Online, catholic.org, accessed March
      27, 2021.

83   Aquinas, *Summa Theologica* III.72.6.

84   Aquinas, III.72.10.

85   St. Patrick's *Confessio* in *St. Patrick: His Confession and Other
      Works*, trans. Fr. Neil Xavier O'Donoghue (New Jersey: Catholic Book
      Publishing, 2009), 26.

86   St. Patrick's *Confessio*, 18–19.

87   *Tripartite Life* in Rev. James O'Leary, D.D., ed., *The Most Ancient Lives
      of Saint Patrick,* 7th ed. (Sound Bend, IN: St. Augustine Academy
      Press, 2010), 98.

88   Recommended reading: I featured St. Patrick (along with Sts. Brigid
      and Kevin) in *Three Irish Saints: A Guide to Finding Your Spiritual*

Style (TAN Books, 2012). For Patrick's story in his own words, see his aforementioned *Confessio,* and for a wealth of fascinating legends consult *The Most Ancient Lives of St. Patrick.*

89 Aquinas, *Summa Theologica* II-II.161.1.

90 Aquinas, II-II.81.5; emphasis added.

91 Antony Flew and Roy Abraham Varghese, *There Is a God: How the World's Most Notorious Atheist Changed His Mind* (New York: HarperOne, 2008), 93, 157.

92 Aquinas, *Summa Theologica* I.2.3.

93 CCC 36, quoting Vatican Council I, *Dei Filius* 2.

94 R. Garrigou-Lagrange, *The Theological Virtues*, vol. 1, *On Faith* (St. Louis: B. Herder, 1965), 114.

95 See, for example, recent data on the Beck Hopelessness Scale first constructed in 1974: Michela Balsamo et al., "Further Insights into the Beck Hopelessness Scale (BHS): Unidimensionality Among Psychiatric Inpatients," *Frontiers in Psychology* 11 (2020): 727, ncbi.nlm.nih.gov.

96 Aquinas, *Summa Theologica* Supp.69.3.

97 Aquinas, I-II.40.7.

98 Aquinas, II-II.23.8, 1.

99 See my book entitled *The One-Minute Aquinas: The Doctor's Quick Answers to Fundamental Questions* (Manchester, NH: Sophia Institute Press, 2014), 83.

100 Aquinas, *Summa Theologica*, II-II.27.7.

101 Aquinas, II-II.27.7.

102 Aquinas, II-II.24.6.

103 *On the Trinity* 8.8, as cited in Aquinas, *Summa Theologica* II-II.25.2.

104 Aquinas, *Summa Theologica* II-II.25.2.

105 Indeed, my own book on the subject, *The Catholic Guide to Loneliness*, was published in 2017.

106   For a recent example showing US and international numbers, see the *Social Pro* article "US Loneliness Statistics and Data 2021," socialpronow.com.

107   *Aquinas Prayer Book*, 33.

108   The acts of faith, hope, and love are found in *United States Catholic Catechism for Adults* (Washington, DC: United States Conference of Catholic Bishops, 2006), 533–534, usccb.org.

109   "Prayer of Saint Richard of Chichester," loyolapress.com.

110   Luciana Frassati, *A Man of the Beatitudes: Pier Giorgio Frassati* (San Francisco: Ignatius, 2001), 57.

111   Recommended reading: Pier Giorgio's sister's book has already been referenced. If you might enjoy a fictionalized account of his life, see Brian Kennelly's *To the Heights: A Novel Based on the Life of Blessed Pier Giorgio Frassati* (Charlotte, NC: Saint Benedict Press, 2014).

112   da Bergamo, *Humility of Heart*, 202.

113   *The Books of the Morals of St. Gregory the Pope, or An Exposition on the Book of Blessed Job*, 3.6.31.87, lectionarycentral.com.

114   Aquinas, *Summa Theologica* II-II.148.1.

115   Aquinas, II-II.148.4.

116   See, for example, the proabortion Guttmacher Institute's July 2020 article "Unintended Pregnancy and Abortion Worldwide," www.guttmacher.org.

117   St. John Climacus, *The Ladder of Divine Ascent*, trans. Colm Luibheid and Norman Russell (Mahwah, NJ: Paulist Press, 1982), 173.

118   St. John Climacus, 176.

119   Aquinas, *Summa Theologica* II-II.118.1.

120   For more information about all of the death-dealing "daughters" of the seven deadly sins and some advice on how to fight them, see my book *The Seven Deadly Sins: A Thomistic Guide to Vanquishing Vice and Sin* (Manchester, NH: Sophia Institute Press, 2015). I refer to this book throughout the chapter.

121   Seneca, *Letters from a Stoic* (New York: Penguin Books, 1969), 34.

122   "Fight for Mansoul," in *Prudentius*, trans. H. J. Thomson (Cambridge, MA: Harvard University Press, 2006), 1.321.

123   *The Seven Deadly Sins*, chap. 14, Kindle.

124   "On Anger," in Seneca, *Moral Essays*, trans. John W. Basore (Cambridge, MA: Harvard University Press, 2003), 1.107, 169.

125   Marcus Aurelius, *Meditations* 2.1.

126   Aquinas, *Summa Theologica*, II-II.35.4.

127   As noted by St. Thomas in *Summa Theologica* II-II.35.4.

128   Aquinas, *Summa Theologica* II-II.161.1.

129   Venerable Louis of Grenada, *The Sinner's Guide* (Charlotte, NC: TAN Books, 2014), chap. 33, books.google.com.

130   Aquinas, *Summa Theologica* II-II.132.1.

131   St. Francis de Sales, *Introduction to the Devout Life: A Popular Abridgment* (Rockford, IL: TAN Books, 1990), 126.

132   "Fight for Mansoul," 1.293.

133   *The Seven Deadly Sins*, conclusion, Kindle.

134   I shared this reflection about the Our Father online at Catholic Exchange several years ago in an article entitled "Christ's Prayer to Conquer the Seven Deadly Sins, " February 11, 2016, catholicexchange.com.

135   *Dialogue of St. Catherine of Siena*, 134.

136   *Dialogue of St. Catherine of Siena*, 134.

137   *Dialogue of St. Catherine of Siena*, 135.

138   Recommended reading: St. Catherine's masterpiece, *The Dialogue of St. Catherine of Siena*; and the biography written by her friend and confessor, Blessed Raymond of Capua, *The Life of St. Catherine of Siena* (Charlotte, NC: TAN Books, 2011).

139   Aquinas, *Summa Theologica* III.57.6.

140   *St. Benedict's Rule for Monasteries*, trans. Leonard J. Doyle
       (Collegeville, MN: Liturgical Press, 1948; Project Gutenberg, 2021),
       chap. 7, gutenberg.org.

141   The wording here comes from their presentation in the *Summa
       Theologica* II-II.161.6. They are listed here in St. Benedict's original
       order. Fr. J. Augustine Wetta, O.S.B. sums up the twelve steps nicely
       in one or two words each as follows: "1. Fear of God, 2. Self-Denial,
       3. Obedience, 4. Perseverance, 5. Repentance, 6. Serenity, 7. Self-
       Abasement, 8. Prudence, 9. Silence, 10. Dignity, 11. Discretion, 12.
       Reverence" in *Humility Rules: Saint Benedict's Twelve-Step Guide to
       Genuine Self-Esteem* (San Francisco: Ignatius, 2017), Contents.

142   Augustine, *On Virginity* 52, as cited in Aquinas, *Summa Theologica* II-
       II.161.6.

143   See, for instance, Aquinas, *Summa Theologica* I.1.8.

144   *St. Benedict's Rule for Monasteries*, chap. 34.

145   Many Christmases my wife and I treat the adults in the family to
       Kentucky bourbon fudge made at the famous Trappist Abbey of
       Gethsemani, where the monks take a vow of silence. Some of the
       batches of fudge really pack a delightful punch. We joke that if one
       monk is adding a little too much bourbon, no one can tell him to stop!

146   As cited in my *How to Think Like Aquinas* (Manchester, NH: Sophia
       Institute Press, 2018), 17–18.

147   Murray, *The New Wine of Dominican Spirituality*, 47–48.

148   Aquinas, *Summa Theologica* II-II.168.4.

149   *St. Benedict's Rule for Monasteries*, chap. 7.

150   *St. Benedict's Rule for Monasteries*, chap. 7.

151   *St. Benedict's Rule for Monasteries*, chap. 7.

152   "La Beata Umiltà: Contemplating on Holy Humility," accessed January
       26, 2022, umilta.net.

153   (Her name is "Humilitas" in Latin.) "La Beata Umiltà," umilta.net. All
       direct quotations in this essay, by the way, come from the same article.

154   Recommend reading: I'm not aware of any biographies of St.
       Humilitas, but interested readers can find various short articles
       through searching her name on the Internet (as I did for the article
       cited within our story).

155   From the *Dicta Anselmi*, chap. 1, as presented in Gregory Sadler,
       "Anselm on the Seven Levels of Humility," *Orexis Dianoētikē* (blog),
       April 11, 2011, gbsadler.blogspot.com. (If you'll forgive my perhaps
       vainglorious name-dropping, it was with great delight that I chanced
       upon this article. Dr. Sadler is a friend of mine, and I had no idea he'd
       written this before we'd met!) Another online resource that digs deep
       into St. Anselm's writings on humility is this one: Austen Haynes, "St.
       Anselm and the Mountain of Humility," *Perfectihabia* (blog), October 9,
       2020, monadshavenowindows.wordpress.com.

156   Aquinas, *Summa Theologica*, II-II.161.6. Quotes from St. Thomas in
       this chapter are from this article, unless otherwise noted.

157   As presented in Sadler, "Anselm on the Seven Levels of Humility."
       This applies to all the quotations from Anselm in the remainder of this
       chapter, unless otherwise noted.

158   Cited in Aquinas, *Summa Theologica* II-II.161.6.

159   Epictetus, *The Handbook*, trans. Nicholas P. White (Indianapolis:
       Hackett, 1983), 13.

160   Excerpt from a prayer of St. Anselm presented as "A Prayer for
       Friends," Pilgrim: A Journal of Catholic Experience (website), accessed
       January 27, 2022, pilgrimjournal.com.

161   Spoken during St. Martin's canonization Mass in 1962.

162   *Capparis spinosa*, whose flowerbuds are used as a tasty seasoning.

163   As told in my *Hounds of the Lord: Great Dominican Saints Every
       Catholic Should Know* (Manchester, NH: Sophia Institute Press, 2015),
       186–187.

164   Recommended Reading: There are many excellent books about St.
       Martin. I have written a chapter about him in *Hounds of the Lord*,
       as cited above—and also about St. Albert the Great, St. Catherine
       of Siena, and Blessed Pier Giorgio Frassati, who are featured in our
       Humility Lived Saint Stories. My main source for the "little stories"
       of St. Martin was Alex García-Rivera, *Saint Martín de Porres: The*

"Little Stories" and the Semiotics of Culture" (Maryknoll, NY: Orbis Books, 1995).

165   Aquinas, *Summa Theologica* I.8.3; emphasis added.

166   From St. Albert the Great's *Mariale or 230 Questions Concerning the Virgin Mary* as cited in Rev. Robert J. Buschmiller, *The Maternity of Mary in the Mariology of St. Albert the Great*, dissertation (University of Fribourg, Switzerland, 1959), 30.

167   With the exceptions, per Aquinas, of the virtues of faith and hope. We read in Hebrews 11:1, "Now faith is the assurance of things hoped for, the conviction of things not seen," and as is said of Christ in John 21:17: "Lord, you know everything." Faith and hope pertain to things unseen. Jesus didn't need them, because he already saw all. (Aquinas, *Summa Theologica* III.7.3, 4). As we saw in chapter 3, neither will we need them when we see God face-to-face in heaven.

168   Aquinas, *Summa Theologica* III.42.4, citing Matthew 7:29: "For he taught them as one who had authority, and not as their scribes."

169   As cited in Aquinas, *Summa Theologica* II-II.161.2.

170   Psalm 132:1 reads, "Remember, O Lord, in David's favor, his humility" in the Revised Standard Version–Second Catholic Edition.

171   In St. Thomas Aquinas, *Commentary on the Gospel of St. Matthew*, trans. Rev. Paul M. Kimball (Dolorosa Press, 2012), 419. The portion of Isaiah 66:2 quoted here reads, "But this is the man to whom I will look, he that is humble and contrite in spirit" in the Revised Standard Version–Second Catholic Edition.

172   St. Thomas More, *The Sadness of Christ: And Final Prayers and Benedictions*, trans. Clarence Miller (New York: Scepter, 1993), 16. (Also cited in my *Catholic Guide to Loneliness* (Manchester, NH: Sophia Institute Press, 2017), 113.)

173   Aquinas, *Summa Theologica* III.75.1.

174   Aquinas, III.75.1.

175   Aquinas, III.75.4–8.

176   Aquinas III.75.1. In the Revised Standard Version–Second Catholic Edition, we read "This is my body which is given for you" (Luke 22:19).

177 Aquinas, III.75.4.

178 St. Thomas Aquinas, *Commentary on the Gospel of St. Matthew*, 419.

179 St. Thomas Aquinas, *Catena Aurea*, vol. 1 – part II, *The Gospel of St. Matthew*, trans. John Henry Newman (New York, NY: Cosimo Classics, 2007), chap. 11.

180 *Catena Aurea*, chap. 11. The Bible verse referenced is Matthew 7:14: "For the gate is narrow and the way is hard, that leads to life."

181 Aelred of Rievaulx, *The Mirror of Charity,* trans. Elizabeth Connor (Kalamazoo, MI: Cistercian Publications, 1990), 133.

182 John Paul II, *Fides et Ratio* (September 14, 1998), vatican.va.

183 As cited in Mary Carruthers, *The Book of Memory: A Study of Memory in Medieval Culture* (New York: Cambridge University Press, 1990), 6.

184 Victor White, *How to Study: Being the Letter of St. Thomas Aquinas to Brother John, De Modo Studendi* (Oxford: Oxonian Press, 1953), 23.

185 For a deep but accessible study of Jesus' own prayer life and how we can strive to make ours like his, I can heartily recommend Shane Kapler's *Through, With, and In Him: The Prayer Life of Jesus and How to Make It Our Own* (Kettering, OH: Angelico Press, 2014).

186 Aquinas, *Aquinas Catechism*, 164.

187 Cited from St. Albert's *Mariale* in *Saint Albertus Magnus* (Racine, WI: Saint Catherine's Press, 1939), 19.

188 Aquinas, *Aquinas Catechism*, 163–165.

189 *Aquinas Catechism*, 165.

190 From Rev. Robert J. Buschmiller, *The Maternity of Mary in the Mariology of Saint Albert the Great*, 27, citing from Albert's *De Naturi Boni (On the Nature of the Good)*.

191 Aquinas, *Aquinas Catechism*, 165.

192 Recommend reading: There have been countless wonderful books written in honor of our Blessed Mother. Of those mentioned in our story above, Rev. Robert J. Buschmiller's, *The Maternity of Mary in the Mariology of Saint Albert the Great* is out of print and may be difficult to track down. Easily accessible, however, are St. Thomas' insights

on the Blessed Mother and the Hail Mary prayer in *The Aquinas Catechism* from Sophia Institute Press.

193   The Very Reverend Adolphe Tanquerey, *The Spiritual Life: A Treatise on Ascetical and Mystical Theology* (Rockford, IL: TAN Books, 2000), 545.

194   I loosely patterned this prayer after St. Thomas Aquinas' prayer "To Acquire the Virtues" in *Aquinas Prayer Book*, 32–39.

195   Attributed to Rafael Merry del Val (1865–1930), cardinal and secretary of state under Pope St. Pius X.

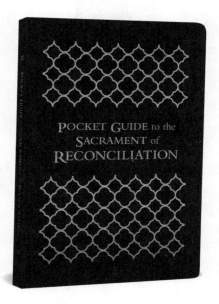